The Beginner's Guide to Wealth

NOEL WHITTAKER
JAMES WHITTAKER

*To the young people of the world:
our future depends on you.*

Other bestsellers by Noel Whittaker:
MAKING MONEY MADE SIMPLE
MORE MONEY WITH NOEL WHITTAKER
LIVING WELL IN RETIREMENT
GOLDEN RULES OF WEALTH
CONTROLLING YOUR CREDIT CARDS
SUPERANNUATION MADE SIMPLE
SHARES MADE SIMPLE
LOANS MADE SIMPLE
DRIVING SMALL BUSINESS
BORROWING TO INVEST
MONEY TIPS
SUPERANNUATION MADE EASY
WINNING PROPERTY TAX STRATEGIES
SAVING TAX ON YOUR INVESTMENT PROPERTY
AGED CARE. WHO CARES?
25 YEARS OF WHITT & WISDOM
RETIREMENT LIVING HANDBOOK
DOWNSIZING MADE SIMPLE
10 SIMPLE STEPS TO FINANCIAL FREEDOM

Other bestsellers by James Whittaker:
THINK AND GROW RICH: THE LEGACY
ANDREW CARNEGIE'S MENTAL DYNAMITE

THE BEGINNER'S GUIDE TO WEALTH
First published in Australia in 2010.
This edition published in 2023 by Noel Whittaker Holdings Pty Ltd.

 A catalogue record for this
book is available from the
NATIONAL
LIBRARY National Library of Australia
OF AUSTRALIA

ISBN 978-0-6458216-3-5 (pbk)

Cover design by Sharon Felschow
Cartoons by Paul Lennon
Typeset in Australia by dta studio, Brendale, Queensland, 4500
Printed in Australia by McPherson's Printing Group, Victoria

10 9 8 7 6 5 4 3 2 1

About the authors

International bestselling author, finance and investment expert, radio broadcaster, newspaper columnist, and public speaker, Noel Whittaker is one of the world's foremost authorities on personal finance.

Noel reaches over four million readers each week through his columns in major Australian newspapers in Sydney, Melbourne, Perth, and Brisbane. He is a contributor to various magazines and websites, and appears regularly on radio and television.

Noel is one of Australia's most successful authors, with 22 bestselling books achieving worldwide sales of more than two million copies. His first book, *Making Money Made Simple*, set Australian sales records and was named in the 100 Most Influential Books of the Twentieth Century.

For 30 years, Noel was a Director of Whittaker Macnaught, one of Australia's leading financial advisory companies, with more than two billion dollars under management. He relinquished all interests in that business in 2007.

In 2011 he was made a Member of the Order of Australia for service to the community in raising awareness of personal finance.

Noel is now an Adjunct Professor with the Queensland University of Technology and a member of the Australian Securities and Investment Commission (ASIC) consumer liaison committee.

James Whittaker is a three-time bestselling author, award-winning entrepreneur, and host of the *Win the Day with James Whittaker* podcast.

After a successful 10-year career in financial planning—where he ran an adviser team with more than $2 billion under management—James began his own entrepreneurial journey. Today, he has launched successful products and companies in dozens of different industries.

James' superpower is helping ambitious but frustrated people gain immediate clarity on what they want and give them a bulletproof plan to achieve it. Through his podcast, media commitments, and social media channels, he helps 2 million people each month to Win the Day®, and has personally coached Olympic gold medallists, billion-dollar founders and CEOs, and special forces operators.

James has been featured extensively in television, print, and digital media around the world, including *The Australian*, *The Today Show*, and *Entrepreneur*. He has also appeared on 600+ podcast and radio shows, spoken to audiences of 2,000+ people, and is a keynote speaker with *Success Magazine*.

His second book, *Think and Grow Rich: The Legacy*, was released in 2018 and has been translated into 15+ languages. It also serves as the official companion to the multimillion-dollar film based on Napoleon Hill's timeless classic. (James is a proud co-executive producer of the film.) His third book, *Andrew Carnegie's Mental Dynamite*, was released in conjunction with the Napoleon Hill Foundation.

Obsessed with what separates ordinary people from extraordinary achievers, James has interviewed over 500 of the world's most revered entrepreneurs, athletes, and changemakers to unlock their secrets to success. In 2022, he was named in the '40 Under Forty in Podcasting' global list by *Podcast Magazine*.

Above all, he hopes to instill the important fundamental truth that each day, if we do not make the decision to win, we have automatically made the decision to lose.

Contents

Introduction

Since its release in 1987 *Making Money Made Simple* has become recognised as the standard work for people who wish to learn the principles of saving and investing money. Seldom a day passes that I don't receive at least one letter or email telling me how that book has changed somebody's life.

I became used to comments of "Why don't they teach this in schools?" or "I wish I had read this when I was young" but gradually I began to realise that young people had a special need—a book written especially for them to show them where to start. After all, you have to learn to make money before you can manage it.

The resolve to write such a book strengthened when I was at a 21st birthday party for the daughter of a friend. During the evening I started chatting with a group of bright young people—the kind of men and women you would expect to be our future leaders. To my amazement they feared the future, were scared at the prospect of trying to find a job and were concerned about their ability to handle the challenges that life will undoubtedly present to them. I left thinking "If these people feel like this, what must the others be going through?"

Soon afterwards, in unrelated incidents, two couples who were clients of our company suffered the trauma of having a teenage child commit suicide. There was no warning or obvious reason, in either case.

A teenage suicide is a tragic waste of an important life and these incidents reinforced my belief that many of our young people are experiencing feelings of confusion and inadequacy as they try to cope with the challenges of a new era dominated by technology and a drive for efficiency at all costs. While these feelings are understandable, it is true that every generation has had its difficulties and the techniques for personal growth and achievement that have worked before will continue to work now.

The aim of this book is to show you how to approach the challenges that lie ahead and to guide you into a success pattern instead of a failure pattern. The road to success can be tough, but those who are prepared will find there are boundless opportunities waiting to be taken. As the great inventor Thomas Edison said, "If we did all the things we are capable of doing we would literally astound ourselves". The recipe for wealth is quite simple: you just need to be earning more than you are spending so you have money left over to invest. Once you can do that, it's only a matter of investing the surplus wisely. This book will show you how to improve your skills to increase your income and then explain simple strategies to make your money work for you.

I am delighted that my son James has co-authored this book with me. He is now a world leader in the field of success and brings an insight to the book that I could not have achieved on my own.

Our wish for you is that you will approach the future with confidence instead of fear and that you will astound yourself at what you find you can do. The future of our world depends on it.

NOEL WHITTAKER

Acknowledgements

When you write a book you appreciate the value of teamwork. We are grateful for the input of many talented and enthusiastic people who happily gave their time to shape *The Beginner's Guide to Wealth* into what you are reading today. A special thank you is due to Noel's wife Geraldine for the hours she spent debating the content of each chapter; to Helena Bond for the editing, Sharon Felschow for cover design and typesetting, and to Paul Lennon for the illustrations.

1

Put on your running shoes

*You only pass through this life once;
you don't come back for an encore.*
Elvis Presley

Young people today face a radically different world from the one in which their parents grew up. The remarkable technological advances in the last 50 years coupled with changes in social attitudes have given many people vastly improved living standards. Nowadays we use the internet or television to watch events as they happen around the world. Computers have taken much of the drudgery out of office work, miracle drugs have improved our life expectancy, heavy machinery has replaced backbreaking work, and discrimination because of gender or race is becoming less common.

However, every action has an opposite reaction. Because computers, robots and AI (artificial intelligence) are doing a larger share of the routine jobs, we achieve a higher output with fewer staff. People are living longer because of medical breakthroughs and improved health care facilities but this all needs funding. As job availability shrinks and more people join the unemployment queues, those taxpayers left in the workforce have to provide funds for a larger welfare bill. Fortunately, both Australia and the US have recently enjoyed a low unemployment rate, but the real test will be whether this is sustainable.

Technology is rapidly transforming the world from an industrial economy to an information-driven economy. Production, administrative and clerical jobs will become scarce as the transformation continues. To make matters worse, our major businesses will not hesitate to outsource their operations if conditions are more favourable somewhere else in the world.

For business managers now, the buzzwords are "efficiency, productivity and customer focus". In simple language, that says they want to look after their customers better but use fewer staff to do it. This means there will be fewer jobs available and more people trying to get them. The bad news is that it's getting tougher out there; the good news is that there's an abundance of outstanding opportunities everywhere for those who are ready.

To take advantage of the opportunities that lie ahead, you will have to learn how to make the right choices in your life. You can choose to handle the future in one of two ways:

(1) Complain about how unfair things have become, give up trying, and despair of ever getting anywhere in such a difficult and changing world.

or

(2) Take the situation as a challenge and make the best of it.

Certainly the world is changing and you face a different set of problems from those your parents and grandparents had to cope with. But remember they also had problems — they just differed from yours. Epictetus, a Greek slave who became a respected and influential philosopher, famously said, "It's not what happens to you, but how you react to it that matters."

As we start you on your journey to success, you need to be aware that people have always faced challenges and that you are lucky to be living where you are now. Imagine if you lived in an overcrowded Third World country, or had been born to poor parents 200 years ago and were working in a mine or a factory at the age of nine.

While every age has, and will have, its own challenges, there is another factor to think about. There have always been some who used the challenges as springboards to success. To do this they adopted some simple, universal and timeless principles that we will teach you in the chapters that follow.

We promise you these principles are **not** hard to understand and they will lead you to a successful life. All you have to do is follow them. That may sound a promise from Hogwarts but it will happen. You can be among the few lucky ones because most people never learn these principles and, many of those who do, never make the effort to put them into practice. As you read you will come across names like Napoleon Hill, Og Mandino, Brené Brown, Denis Waitley, Samuel Smiles, Wayne Dyer and Jim Rohn. These are people who have inspired the world. There is more information about them at the back of the book.

Now might be an appropriate time for a story. It sounds at first like just a joke but it has a message that's really worth thinking about.

Two people were hiking through the jungle when they heard the sound of a tiger nearby. Both were terrified but one stopped and started to put on a pair of running shoes. "What do you think you are doing?" said the other. "You know you can't outrun a tiger no matter what you are wearing on your feet."

"I don't have to outrun the tiger," was the response. "I only have to beat you!"

That's the way the world is going. The gap between the "haves" and the "have nots" will widen as jobs become harder to get and the work available splits further into skilled and unskilled. You can put on your running shoes safe in the knowledge that over 80% of the population will worry about what is happening yet will do nothing to improve their situation. It is the minority who will take action, such as reading this book, and change their lives for the better.

As this book is probably your introduction to the subject of success, we have tried to make it an easy read for you. Most of the chapters are short and they each have one major message that is repeated continually to imprint it on your mind. At the end of each chapter you will have to decide if you want to keep on going or "opt out". It's a bit like the TV game show where the player has the choice of taking the money now or coming back next week to win more. There is just one difference with this book — the chapters don't get any harder. If you can follow one you can follow the next.

Make your first choice now. If you are not interested in improving your life, stop here and give the book to somebody else. However, if you want to make the most of the potential you have, and the tremendous opportunities you have been given, put on your running shoes and read on.

Key points:

- Take each situation as a challenge and make the best of it.
- It's not what happens to you but how you react to it that matters.
- Increase your skills to become one of the "haves".
- Put on your running shoes!

2

It's not an accident

*I didn't get there by wishing for it, or
hoping for it, but by working for it.*

Estée Lauder

The message of this chapter is that success in life is a
decision, not an accident of birth or a lucky break.
Your future depends on the actions you take from now on.
What you have done in the past is of no importance.

You are reading this book because:

(1) Somebody gave it to you

or

(2) You bought it for yourself.

If somebody gave it to you, they must have thought that
reading the book would give you some clues to a happier
life. That's a great advantage.

If you bought it for yourself, deep down you probably feel
the itch of frustration—a feeling that life is like a beautiful
valley waiting for you once you cross the mountain. The
problem is that the mountain looks forbidding and there
are many well-worn trails at the bottom of it. You've tried
a few that didn't take you anywhere and you're reaching

a stage where you're scared to try many more in case you discover that none of them will take you anywhere either. That's how so many of us feel. You could sum it up by saying you've got a feeling you could really be something if only you knew where to begin.

Read on. This book will start you on the right path and help you unlock some of that potential stored inside you. Congratulate yourself for being courageous enough to start taking charge of your future.

Living on biscuits

We'll start with a story about a young couple:

They had spent years living frugally to get enough money for a house deposit, and finally, the great day arrived when their deposit was enough to get approval for a home loan. They decided to celebrate by having a holiday.

They booked a 14-day boat cruise but spent so much money on the tickets that there was little left over for spending money. To overcome the problem, and to keep their spare money for shopping, they worked out a plan to save money on meals. They bought a box of crackers and baked beans and, instead of dining in the ship's restaurant, ate biscuits and beans for breakfast, lunch, and dinner in their cabin.

They got very tired of baked beans, but the weather was great, the company was fine, and they had the best holiday of their lives. On the final night of the cruise, they carefully counted how much spending money remained and decided they could afford to break out and eat their final dinner in the ship's dining room.

They got all dressed up and prepared for a memorable evening. However, when they arrived at the plush dining room they were puzzled when the head waiter escorted them to a superb table and handed them the huge men-us because there were no prices shown. When they asked why, the waiter replied, "Of course there are no prices — the meals are included in the cost of the fare!"

They had spent the whole trip on a starvation diet of crackers and beans because they had not realised the meals were included. What a waste!

Life is like that. Most people go through life living on the equivalent of crackers and beans because they never knew how much else was available. A fortunate few learn the lesson when young — as I hope you will — and some, like Noel, do not learn it until they are 35. The majority never learn it at all.

James says...

Humans, as a whole, have undergone more changes in the last century than we have in all previous centuries since the dawn of time. We are becoming a society reliant on energy drinks and junk food, wasting away in front of mobile devices and gaming consoles, and sourcing pleasure from areas that don't always assist in our personal growth and development.

Sure, these things can be fun — in moderation — but anymore than that and it becomes a negative routine that can be difficult to break out of. It's easy to fall into this routine, and that's why so many of us do it.

These habits, as well as our evolutionary hardwiring, have also created a more anxious society, as the gap between what we did thousands of years ago is replaced by modern living.

If you're not feeling the excitement of accomplishment on a regular basis, prioritise your hours and then reflect — do you have potential that's going to waste?

Success is for you

The message of this chapter is that success is available for you — if you know how to achieve it. Right now you may be thinking "It's all right for somebody like Noel to talk about success, he has never experienced the problems I have".

Noel says...

Let me tell you a little about my background. My father managed a pig farm and I went to a small country school. When the farm was sold, we found ourselves with no home because we had always lived on the farm in the manager's house. My father was out of a job and the only place he could find work was as a labourer in a foundry.

I was so clumsy at school that the manual arts teacher would hold up my pathetic efforts at woodwork for all the class to laugh at. I was dropped from most of the health and physical education classes and never made a sporting team. When I finished high school I decided I was too dumb to go to university and, instead, joined a bank because it was a long-established institution. For the first 35 years of my life I suffered with a massive inferiority complex and did not start to realise my potential until I read Think and Grow Rich *by Napoleon Hill. My life was transformed from that moment.*

The main reason I wrote Making Money Made Simple *was to save people all those years I wasted. The reason for writing the book you are now holding was to get a similar message across to people but in a way that is specially tailored to the young so they can put the principles into practice sooner.*

You **must** understand that success in life is not dependent on what your background is, what has happened to you in the past, how brainy you are, how good looking you are or how much luck comes your way. Sure, some people do seem to get a great start in life because of some special talent or circumstances but for the rest of us **there is always a compensating factor**. In fact, many gifted people find everything all too easy at first and never learn the important habits of persistence and patience. Having wealthy parents can be more of a hindrance than a help. Children of the so-called "wealthy and glamorous" movie stars or members of the royal family have certainly had their fair share of problems, and made worse because they're often made very public (as you can see everywhere in the media).

Many young people from poor backgrounds discover that this provides the spur for them to do better than their parents. They may not have done as well in life if they had come from privileged backgrounds. Others learned from a tough background. Musician Anthony Kiedis (Red Hot Chili Peppers), talk show host Oprah Winfrey, and rugby league coach Wayne Bennett are just a few who endured significant personal hardship at a young age before fighting their way to the pinnacle of their chosen field.

In fact, coming from wealthy parents may well be a disadvantage as studies have shown that only a small number of family businesses survive to the third generation. The process goes like this:

(1) The grandparents start to build a business from scratch. They pick up the necessary skills along the way and most of what they learn is from experience.

(2) The next generation learns directly from the founders and, when the founders die, take over a thriving business. However, the founders had the unique experience of building from nothing, whereas the second generation received help from their parents when the inevitable business problems occurred.

(3) The members of the third generation are born to wealth and are too often protected by their parents from the chance to learn. Because the grandchildren never had the chance to learn the skills of their parents and grandparents, they are unable to handle the problems of the now large business and it may go into decline or be sold. The third generation often ends up broke.

This has given rise to the expression: "Shirt sleeves to shirt sleeves in three generations".

So forget about using your background as an excuse and remember that we all have potential we can put to use. In this book we will show you that success in life is predictable and that it can almost always be achieved if you follow certain rules. Therefore there are two major steps: learn what has to be done, and then put it into practice. You can do it if **you want to**.

Key points:

- Your future depends on the actions you take from now on.
- Success is available for you — if you know how to achieve it.
- Many gifted people find everything all too easy at first and never learn the important habits of persistence and patience.
- Ignore your background — we all have potential we can put to use.
- Learn what has to be done, and then put it into practice.
- Your success will directly correlate with how much time you're willing to commit to it.

3
Success —
What is it?

I want to be all that I am capable of becoming.
Katherine Mansfield

The aim of this book is to help you to become a "success". Therefore, in this chapter we'll think about what the word means.

Becoming "successful" is a bit like becoming "happy"; the words have different meanings for everybody. One dictionary defines success as "the accomplishment of an aim" and "good fortune". Earl Nightingale describes success as "the realisation of a worthy goal". You will have to find your own definition, but personally we regard successful people as those who are in control of their life, who are working at what they enjoy, and who are contributing to society.

Think of your life as travelling in a car. You can choose to be in the driver's seat, deciding where to go, how fast to go, and when to take a break. This involves planning the route, keeping a watch on the road ahead, and allowing for events such as hail storms, accidents or road blocks that may hold you up. You are also responsible for putting the fuel in the car and paying for the repairs. You experience both the pleasure and the responsibility. You are in charge.

You can choose to be a passenger in which case you will have no say over where the car goes and you will just have to hope it travels in the direction that you want to go. There is no need to look out the window or to plan ahead. You can stay safely inside and be at the mercy of somebody else's decisions and never have any say in your life. Whether you choose to be a driver or a passenger is up to you but according to our definition, successful people are the ones who have taken control of their life and are living it on their terms. They are in the driver's seat.

Just be aware that it is possible to be a success in one area of your life and not in another. This is called being "out of balance". A common example is the business executive who works long hours and is probably considered highly successful at work but who neglects health and family and thus spends most of the time suffering extreme pressure. The outcome is often a physical and mental breakdown coupled with the realisation, too late, that they have missed most of the true joys of life.

Success to us is:

- Working at a job you enjoy instead of one you hate.

- Owning your own home so you are not at the mercy of a landlord who may force you to move out.

- Having the financial freedom to travel and experience the wonders of our unique world.

- Having fulfilling and happy personal relationships instead of living in conflict.

- Freedom to choose. Not only is it a great feeling to be able to choose what you buy based on what you want rather than what you can afford, it also enables you to contribute to the causes you care about most.

- Feeling good about yourself.
- Having a well-rounded life so you enjoy a range of activities.

We promise you that if you follow what is in this book, you will have a better life, you will be financially secure, you will wake up on most mornings looking forward to the day, you will have happy relationships and you will feel good about yourself. You will also discover some incredible powers within yourself. We are not promising you total freedom from problems or stress, but if you follow the principles in this book you will find they are a part of life that you will take in your stride.

Giving up to get

This is a good time to tell you about another important concept — to move forward you must give up. Saving for a home means you have to give up spending all your pay. The reward is the security of owning your own home. Having children means giving up personal freedom for the joy of being a parent. Becoming an adult involves giving up being taken care of in return for being able to make your own decisions. A fit body involves giving up some of the fun of gorging on junk food. Owning your own business means giving up the security of working for somebody else in exchange for the chance to run your own life.

Giving up is a fact of life and none of us can change it. The good news is that you will find that by giving up you can achieve more than you had before. There are great rewards.

In the next chapter you will learn your first lesson — how to avoid the negative pull of those around you.

Key points:

- Find your own definition of "success" but, generally, successful people are the ones who have taken control of their life and are living it on their terms.

- To move forward, you must be prepared to give up less important things to reach a more important goal.

4

Most people

*We forfeit three-fourths of ourselves in
order to be like other people.*

Arthur Schopenhauer

The message of this chapter is that most people never
learn or practise success habits and, as a result, die
without using their potential. They often drift through life
working at jobs they don't enjoy, dreading the thought of
Mondays and, yet, fear the loss of their jobs. They usually
end up living on welfare convinced that life has dealt them
a cruel hand.

In *Making Money Made Simple* Noel discussed research
that had been carried out on typical 16-year-olds.

By the time they are 65:

- 76% of them are either dead or dead broke
- 16% are getting by
- Only 8% — that's one in every 12 — have made it
  financially.

That's a scary lot of figures, but what do they say to you?

It should tell you that most people are doing it wrong.
Now this is an extremely valuable piece of information — if

most are doing it wrong it should follow that if you do what they do, you will be on the wrong track too. Maybe it also follows that doing things **differently** may be a recipe for success.

Author Earl Nightingale claims "Winners do the things that failures aren't prepared to do", while Canadian author Brian Tracy believes "Winners spend their time on activities that produce results, whereas losers spend their time on activities that relieve tension".

Let's think about what most people do and don't do. Most people waste at least 20 hours a week watching mundane television or gaming, and they **never** read books, listen to podcasts or take courses that will improve their mind.

They also can't wait to finish their work at the end of the day, can't wait for Friday to come, never set goals, and spend their whole lives wishing they could win the lottery so they would never have to work again.

In a later chapter you will learn your rewards in life will match your service. Therefore, it should be obvious that those who spend life providing no meaningful service to anybody else will get rewards in keeping with that effort. It may also explain why so many lottery winners who were broke when they won the money are back to being broke a couple of years after the big win.

"What about peer pressure?" we hear you say. "If all my friends are having a good time, why can't I?" Hold it. We have never written anything that suggests people shouldn't have a good time.

But understand there is a time to resist peer pressure. Otherwise you will end up like the majority, which we now know is not all it's cracked up to be.

The aim of this book is to enable you to have the greatest time you could imagine by showing you ways to become more than you ever dreamed of. Be assured — the views are better from the house that overlooks the water.

The great escape

Noel was one of the guest speakers at a convention in Fiji and sat enthralled as a high earning 24-year-old told his story to a large audience. He had been a shearer but found the work hard and the shearing sheds hot. His goal was to break out of those sheds to find a job he enjoyed and to make more money. He told how he would spend night after night reading books like *Think and Grow Rich* and how the other shearers, who were more concerned with drinking, teased him about it.

His reply to them was "One day I'll be out of these shearing sheds and you guys will still be stuck here." The goal of a better life kept him on track and able to withstand the pressure from his workmates who, as far as he knows, are still shearing sheep and wishing they were doing something else.

We know it can be hard to withstand pressure from your fellow human beings, but there are two solutions: you can either lead the group in the direction in which you want to travel, or you can change your circle of friends to one that has goals and dreams that fit with yours.

Example: *Mark wants to lose some weight and get fit. He has difficulty in getting motivated because all his friends eat junk food, and drink too much. However, if Mark joins the local gym he will meet people who are keen to keep fit and healthy, and will probably discover there is just as much fun in going for a run than hanging around bars and clubs.*

Alternatively he could do his friends a service and organise the whole group to go for an early morning run a few times a week. Deep down they would probably all welcome this, but nobody has got around to suggesting it.

We cannot stress enough the power of the people you mix with. We know that people will respond well if you take them out of their environment (work or home), give them a good course with top coaches and teach them a bunch of skills. However, the whole value of the course is generally lost within a few weeks if they return to their old environment and mix with the same negative people. The only solution is to send the whole group to the same course.

The reason for slipping back into the old pattern of behaviour is obvious when you think about it. It takes more effort to climb the mountain than to slip down it, and usually the worst course of action for you is the easiest one. It takes effort to refuse a cigarette when your friends are having one and to say, "I can't afford to go out — I am saving for a home," when everybody is planning a night on the town. It is far simpler to mix with people who have compatible goals with yours. Then you can all agree to have a cheap night out or stay at home and make your own fun.

Tapping in

Another way to resist peer pressure is to be part of what Napoleon Hill called a "mastermind" group. This is a group of people with similar goals who meet with the common purpose of helping one another achieve them. Hill regarded such a group as so important that he devoted the first chapter of his famous book *The Law of Success* to the idea. He states he has proved time and time again that "every human brain is both a broadcasting and a receiving station for vibrations of thought and frequency". He believed the coming together of several minds created a mind that was bigger than all the others put together.

James says...

Many years ago, in the early stages of my professional career, three friends and I decided to form our own mastermind. We committed to meeting regularly where we would tap into our combined knowledge. Our group discussed business ideas and concepts, financial information and investment proposals, and nominated a person each meeting to present their ideas to the group (this allowed us to all improve our public speaking skills too). We were from fairly different industries, but this allowed us to learn about things we weren't so familiar with and enhance our knowledge in areas we did understand.

The group also made a commitment to put away a certain amount of money each month, which we would eventually invest in companies that we had researched ourselves. Although the four of us now live in different corners of the globe, the learnings from that first group are still fresh in my head, and I'll always cherish the lessons we learned much more than the returns on our investments.

In 2013, when I first moved to Los Angeles, I knew forming a similar group would be a huge advantage. The journey has been extremely rewarding, only this time we had six people in an incredible alliance that has seen us adequately equipped to navigate career changes, weddings, children, buying properties and so much more. We even began hosting regular gatherings where we would each invite a few likeminded people so we could expand our networks.

It would be impossible to describe how quickly and purposefully your life changes when you find yourself in an environment like this. The people you're with become the strongest friends you can imagine, and you know they will do anything they can to see you succeed. As everyone's careers begin to develop, that only becomes more potent.

If you nurture it carefully, the power of relationships will be the greatest asset you ever have. Just remember the golden rule of relationships—to GIVE before you get.

Since this book is used as an introduction to a new and exciting world for you, we won't be delving too deeply into the concept of a mastermind. However, you can learn more about it in James' book *Think and Grow Rich: The Legacy* or through his Win the Day Accelerator[1]. As you learn more

---

[1] *https://jameswhitt.com*

about success you will find the concept of a mastermind group comes up regularly and, as your awareness grows, the right people will start to appear in your life. The point we want to get across is the massive power exerted on you by the people you mix with. On many occasions we've been caught up with the excitement and motivation that a determined and inspiring friendship network provides. But it's hard to avoid the pull of less focused and negative people who want to keep you from being all you can be. Make a commitment to put yourself in both of these settings, and observe the different energies that these polar opposite attitudes exude.

It happens because we tend to act like those around us. If they are negative and always blaming everybody else for their problems, they will drag you down too and you will soon start to act the same way.

Fortunately, as you practise the principles in this book, you will find that you automatically move towards people who will help you get where you want to go. There is a Buddhist saying, "When the pupil is ready the teacher will appear", and that has certainly been true for us.

The vibrations of thought that Napoleon Hill wrote about can possibly attract to us the people we need. Maybe a mind that is prepared sees opportunities that are not clear to another mind. Whatever the reason, it works.

Meanwhile don't forget that if you continue to act like the majority you will end up where they end up. Dead broke at 65!

Key points:

- If most people are doing it wrong, then doing what they do could put you on the wrong track too.
- Our rewards in life will match our service.
- You can either lead the group in the direction you want to travel or change your circle of friends to one with goals and dreams like yours.
- It takes more effort to climb the mountain than to slip down it. Usually the worst course of action is the easiest.
- A mastermind group delivers extra power to help you achieve your goals.

5

Starting a chain reaction

It's fine to celebrate success, but it is more important to heed the lessons of failure.
Bill Gates

In this chapter you will learn how to use a magic formula to start a chain reaction that will take you where you want to go.

By now you should know that success is possible for you and understand that it **doesn't** depend on who your parents are, how brainy you are, what you look like, or what you have done so far in your life. It depends on your taking a series of steps that we'll call the "magic formula". We have used the word "magic" because of the extraordinary results that can occur once you start. Actually there is nothing magical about it at all — it's simply the laws of cause and effect operating.

Success depends on a chain reaction that you may well have already started. You take an action that leads to a further action, and then to another action, and finally you get a result that until now you may never have dreamed was possible. There is one catch: the process often takes a long time to work, which is why many who start don't stick with it.

As Brian Tracy explained in *The Psychology of Success*, many studies have shown that success is like baking a cake — if you use the right ingredients and mix them properly, the result is predictable. You can therefore move confidently forward secure in the knowledge that if you follow certain clearly defined steps the results will come.

You are lucky because most of the research has been done for you. Napoleon Hill spent 20 years under the guidance of the famous industrialist, Andrew Carnegie, studying the techniques used by over 100 of the most successful men and women in the world in the early 20th century. They included Henry Ford the car manufacturer, Thomas Edison the inventor and F. W. Woolworth who started the shopping chain.

Hill found that all these people used the magic formula and in 1927 published his findings in his book *The Law of Success*. This was such a large book that he condensed the information into his famous book *Think and Grow Rich* which has been on the bestseller lists for more than 80 years. Every time Noel makes a speech to business people he asks for a show of hands from those who have read *Think and Grow Rich*. Always a lot of hands go up and it becomes obvious that, for so many of the audience, Napoleon Hill's books were the start of their success.

(In 2016, in an incredible twist of fate, the Napoleon Hill Foundation asked James to write a modern companion to *Think and Grow Rich*, which was released to great success as *Think and Grow Rich: The Legacy*. As a result, James has interviewed more than 100 of the world's most accomplished business leaders, cultural icons, and athletes to share their success habits with today's generations. His efforts on that project have led to numerous other collaborations with the Napoleon Hill Foundation, including annotating the book *Andrew Carnegie's Mental Dynamite*. James has a deep sense of duty to keep the Hill legacy alive and introduce it to as many people as possible. You will notice that all of our work is heavily influenced by Hill's timeless wisdom, as well as that of those he influenced through people such as Jim Rohn and Jim Stovall.)

A multitude of books have been devoted to the subject of "success" and we have included the names of some of them in our suggested basic library (at the back of this book) because there is no doubt they have changed hundreds of thousands of lives. It is our heartfelt wish that *The Beginner's Guide to Wealth* will be at the start of your journey, which will include reading many of the other fascinating books on the subject.

Now, let's get down to work. In simple terms, the rules of achievement can be summarised as follows:

(1) You must **believe** you have the ability.

(2) You must make the effort **before** you enjoy the results.

(3) You must set clearly defined **goals**.

(4) You must **increase your value** as a person through continual self-development.

(5) You must have **persistence** and **learn from your failures**.

(6) You must maintain a **positive mental attitude**.

(7) You must take **full responsibility** for your successes and failures.

Now we'll examine each of these factors in detail and you'll learn ways to put them all into practice. It's not difficult but it does take time and work.

As we proceed, remember that being in control is one of the ultimate achievements in life. Think about it. The winners can spend most of each day doing what they choose to do—what makes them happiest. In contrast the losers spend most of their time worrying about money and doing things they don't particularly like because they have no alternative. The choice is yours.

Zero for skill, Fran, but 10 out of 10 for persistence.

Believing you have the ability

For many of you this will be the hardest part but the following techniques will help. There is more in the chapter on self-concept (chapter seven) which shows you how your brain works, gives you methods of changing how you see yourself, and helps you think about what happened to change that unstoppable confidence with which you were born.

Look at any infant and you will see what you once were: fearless, confident, curious about everything on the planet, and with an insatiable demand for learning. No matter how often you fell over, you got up again; no matter how much the adults said, "Don't touch," you persisted. You really were a giant in the making.

Then slowly, and sadly, you began to take notice of "most people" and you started to follow the crowd. Your confidence gave way to fear and that thirst for knowledge slowly ebbed away. It became easier to conform than to be different, and much more comfortable to stagnate watching excessive television than to stretch your brain on a new skill.

The way to regain that confidence is to get it back the way you lost it—little by little. We'll go into it in detail soon.

Making the effort before you enjoy the results

You may think this is obvious but you'll find "most people" don't appreciate it and go through life without making any serious effort and then blaming everybody else for their failures. They have never learned that our rewards are multiplied by our output.

Setting clearly defined goals

Ask any winner what made the difference and they will say, "Goals". Goal setting is of vital importance to success, yet it is rarely taught in schools. "Most people" have never learned how to do it, so we have given it a full chapter in this book. If you follow the techniques set out in this book you will reach a stage where you will be able to achieve any realistic goal you set for yourself. It is estimated that as little as 3% of people set goals, so make sure you're on the good side of that statistic—where winners are made.

Practising continual self-development

This is a major factor because your rewards in life are in proportion to the way you develop your skills and, as the world changes, people with the right skills will be in demand. There is a full chapter in this book on the importance of self-development but if you read between the lines you will notice the entire book is devoted to starting a process that will bring out the hidden potential that is in you now.

Understanding failure

Noel says...

One of my major problems when I was younger was that I never appreciated the effort that went into making a winner. I learned the piano for a few weeks but found it difficult and decided I had no natural ability. Then I bought a saxophone and fiddled with it for a while but never got around to serious practice. I envied the singers and musicians in the movies who could belt out a tune with no apparent effort, but got a rude awakening when I went to hear a well-known singer and orchestra and made a request for a special number. They couldn't play it because "we don't have the music for it". That was the end of my illusions about ad libbing a tune as you see happening in the movies.

It took years before I discovered that those who perform difficult feats with apparent ease have spent years of hard slog to get that way. Everything of value takes time.

Don't let the first defeat put you off trying again. To grow as a person and to develop your skills, you must stretch yourself and try things you have never done before. You would be a most extraordinary person if you could get all these new skills right the first time.

As the American writer and philosopher Elbert Hubbard said, "The greatest mistake a person can make is to be afraid of making one." There is nothing wrong with making a mistake and there is nothing wrong with failing. The only real failure is failing to try. Failure is an integral part of success and it never stopped you when you were a child learning to walk.

Keeping a positive mental attitude

If you have a positive mental attitude you expect the best from every situation. It's a strange quirk in life that we usually get what we expect; therefore it makes sense to always expect good things to happen. Luckily it is simply a habit that comes naturally after a little bit of practice.

Taking full responsibility for your life

The main message of this book is that you can have the most wonderful life if you decide to do what is necessary to achieve it. That statement implies the actions you take from now on will determine your future. As you have the power to control these actions, it must follow that you have the power to control your future. Certainly it takes some effort but, as you will soon discover, the rewards are far greater than the effort.

In his best-selling book, *A Recipe for Dreaming*, author Bryce Courtenay wrote, "It isn't hard at the top. It's easy. It isn't crowded and it's really quite civilised. What's hard is the bottom. Down there you'll find a hundred times more competition. Down there is where people stand on your teeth so that they can get a firmer foot-hold on the first rung of the ladder out of hell. Why then is it that most people seem so afraid of success that they'll do almost anything to avoid it?"

The choice is yours.

Key points:

- Feed your mind and develop your skills.
- Believe in yourself and your own ability.
- Winners can spend most of each day doing what they choose to do.
- Set clearly defined goals so you know where you're heading.
- Understand the value of persistence — everything of value takes time.
- The only real failure is failing to try.
- You can have the most wonderful life if you decide to do what is necessary to achieve it.

6

Reframing: It's how you look at it!

I learned that courage was not the absence of fear, but the triumph over it. The brave man is not he who does not feel afraid, but he who conquers that fear.

Nelson Mandela

The message in this chapter is that you live your life as you see it. Therefore, you can change your life by changing the way you look at it.

You have probably heard the story about two men in a bar arguing about whether a glass of beer was half full or half empty. Of course both are right; it depends on your point of view. However, even though both are right, the person who felt he still had half a glass left may have been far happier than the one who believed that his beer was nearly finished.

As you go through life you will find there are few absolutes and that what you think you see is usually **literally** what you get. Because of this, we will now explain a technique that has enormous potential to help you better your life. It is called "reframing", which means changing the way you look at something.

Understand that you can choose how you think about something. How you think may be influenced by what you have experienced before, what you think you are seeing, or how you have trained yourself to react. Here are some examples.

Noel says...

When I was a brash young 20-year-old I had just joined a golf club. One day I saw the Club President walk up to the first tee accompanied by what appeared to be a tramp. The man was dirty, scruffily dressed and, to make it worse, had trouble hitting the golf ball. The next time I saw the President I asked him why he was lowering the club standards by letting such a person on the course. His answer stunned me. "That man is a friend of mine who lost his wife and children in an accident about a year ago. His doctor thinks golf might help him." The moment I heard that, I could have sunk into the ground, but it immediately reframed the way I saw the situation.

Years ago my wife and I were in Paris and I was operating on the premise that Parisians were very rude because they had seemed that way on my last visit. Naturally I had been rude back to them. My wife convinced me to try thinking of them as pleasant people and to act as if they were. To my amazement, most of the Parisians we met were delightful. What had changed? Only the way my brain was working.

You should now understand that reframing involves how you think about situations and then making a conscious choice about how you will react to them—the best thing about it is that it shifts your focus to problem-solving and positivity.

Let's start with your reaction to unemployment, a topic that is critical to most of us. If 10% of people are out of work you will probably tell yourself that unemployment is 10% and focus on the difficulties that creates. You don't have to think like this. You could mentally reframe it and decide that if 10% are unemployed, 90% of people must have jobs, in which case there must still be plenty of hope. What if youth unemployment reaches 40%? Then is it not still true that 60% (that's nearly two thirds) of our young people **do** have jobs?

We are not playing with words here. You have the choice of seeing it any way you choose. However, the benefit of changing your thinking like this is that you start to get your mind off the worry of unemployment. This enables you to start focusing on ways to make sure you end up in the 60% that have a job, not the 40% who don't. Look around you and listen quietly. You will notice that "most people" waste their time focusing on the problem and never try to find ways to solve it.

Do you remember what we discussed in chapter one? It's not what happens to you, but how you react to it that matters. You cannot change what is. What you can change is the way you respond to it. This will then change the way you act, which will in turn lead you to a more favourable outcome.

We have introduced the concept of reframing early in the book because its understanding is vital to your success. Here are some examples for you to think about to make sure you understand it properly:

(1) A young person breaks up with their boyfriend or girlfriend. The choice is to regard that as the end of the world and mope around for months, or to regard it as an occasion to find somebody else. It may even be an opportunity to take an overseas holiday or find a job somewhere else that may lead to all sorts of exciting possibilities.

(2) A family goes for a holiday to the beach and experiences a week of wet weather. One family might sit around and complain about the weather for a week, another family might see it as a chance to go to the movies, play games and spend time together.

In *The Law of Success* Napoleon Hill uses the reframing concept without giving it a name. He states:

"You are fortunate if you have learned the difference between temporary defeat and failure; more fortunate still, if you have learned the truth that the very seed of success is dormant in every defeat that you experience."

This means if you look hard enough you will find an opportunity in even the worst of happenings.

James says...

In 2014, I had the opportunity to interview one of the most inspirational people I'd ever encountered. Todd Love grew up in Atlanta, Georgia where he was a self-described adrenaline junkie. His father and grandfather were both proud members of the United States

Marine Corps, so Todd continued the family tradition.

During active duty in Afghanistan, with his M4 carbine rifle in his right hand and a metal detector in his left, 20-year-old Todd led his fellow Marines into an empty compound to clear it of threats. Todd stepped on an improvised explosive device (IED) and the blast launched him 15 feet backwards. The IED was made of low metallic copper, which prevented his metal detector from picking it up.

His first memory after the incident was waking up in a hospital in Germany two days later. In a lot of pain, Todd figured that he must've stood on an IED but, due to heavy medication, he didn't realise the extent of his injuries.

Several days later, after being transported to the US for more treatment, Todd said, "I started getting curious and went to grab my leg, but it simply wasn't there. All I felt was the hospital bed." He realised shortly after that **both** his legs had been blown off in the explosion.

One of his hands was wrapped in bandages, and it was so badly destroyed that the doctors recommended amputation at the elbow. Todd concurred with medical opinion, and after the amputation he was left with only one full limb. His life had been literally torn apart.

Tears started to well in my eyes long before this part of the story. Wouldn't it be completely understandable for Todd to hate the world and spend the rest of his life in self-pity? It absolutely would, but Todd won't ever let that *be the case. He is now a skydiving fanatic, and has even completed the Spartan Race, a gruelling obstacle course, on five separate occasions. A simple internet image search for "Todd Love" presents a mosaic of inspiration and courage.*

Todd describes the incident as a "blessing". He explains, "It made me fall in love with life again. Even though I have these obstacles to face, I started properly noticing all the people who I really love and care about. That's what life is about. Everyone is going through something in their life right now. For me, my injuries are obvious, but we all have different obstacles in life that we deal with. The important thing is that we stay positive and focus on what we can control."

You will see reframing everywhere once you become aware of it. Thomas Edison, the inventor of the light bulb, spent years trying to find the secret. Once a reporter asked him how it felt to fail 10,000 times. His answer was "I haven't failed 10,000 times — I now know 10,000 ways not to do it."

A friend of Noel's received a summons for $50,000 for alleged negligence in his business. Instead of ranting and raving about having to fight the action in Court, he took it as a warning that there were defects in his systems that needed fixing. Maybe that summons saved him from a future summons for a much larger amount.

Here's another story.

Two men stopped to buy a magazine. The man behind the counter was one of the rudest people they had ever met. One of the men continued to be pleasant to the paper seller, which prompted his friend to remark, "How can you be nice to such an awful person?" The answer was "You don't think I'm going to let a fool like that control my actions, do you?"

Notice how he kept control of the situation in his own hands and how that changed the way his friend looked at the incident.

Our family used to play a game when we faced a rude person. We would put all our efforts into making that person smile and after a little work we usually succeeded.

Playing "games" goes much further than having fun. By reframing the situation into a challenge and looking at it in a new way, you are transforming yourself into a person who can take control of any situation. No longer are you a robot reacting mindlessly to anybody who wants to press your button — you have changed to a person who is able to control your emotions and take charge.

As you meet successful people in all walks of life you will notice that most of them have the philosophy of "that was meant to be" when an unwanted incident happens. W. Clement Stone, the President of Combined Insurance Inc., greeted all bad news with the words "That's good", and

then he would think about ways to find something good out
of the bad that had happened.

When you reframe a situation you take control of it. By
asking yourself "How can I turn this to my own good?" you
are putting your creative powers to work towards finding
a solution instead of wallowing around complaining like
"most people" do. Suppose you apply for a job, or for a promotion, and miss out. Yes, you have missed out and, for
today, you can't do a single thing to change that. However,
you could analyse why you missed out and plan to do better
next time. It is also possible that missing that opportunity
allows you to take advantage of a better one that is waiting
around the corner.

In his podcast, former US Navy SEAL commander Jocko
Willink mentioned a simple response he used to help reframe the mindset of those under his command. Whenever
one of them would vent to him about an injury, adversity or
challenging circumstance, Willink would respond, "Good!"

On this management style, Willink explained, "When
things are going bad, there's always going to be some good
that comes from it. If you can say the word 'Good,' it means
you're still alive. It means you're still breathing. And if

you're still breathing, then you've still got some fight left in you."

That single word helps reveal the absolute truth that every problem is simply an opportunity to figure out a solution. The more solutions at your disposal, the more valuable you become—whether on the battlefield or in the boardroom.

The ability to reframe a situation in a positive manner will be a critical factor in your search for success. In the next chapter we'll consider how your brain works and how you can start to think highly of yourself.

Key points:

- You can change your life by changing the way you look at it.

- Reframing involves analysing how you think about situations and then making a conscious choice about how you will react to them.

- By reframing the situation into a challenge and looking at it in a new way, you are transforming yourself into a person who can take control of any situation.

7

What do you think about you?

It is not our physical selves that limit us, but rather our mindset about our physical limits.
Dr Ellen Langer

You now know the magic formula for success and understand that the approach you take to life has a huge role in deciding your future. However, knowledge is not enough. To succeed, you must believe that it is possible for you. In this chapter we'll think about the key factor that will make or break you — it's called "self-concept".

How do you genuinely see yourself? Ask a room full of teenagers, or even adults, and you'll probably hear a stack of self-derogatory comments. Words like "average" or "not much". Many will even take it a step further and use terms like "too skinny", "too dumb", "too tall", "too clumsy". There seems to be a feeling in our society that it's wrong to think good things about ourselves. There is also a custom that you show hidden admiration for your friends by saying something nasty about them — to their faces of course.

It's a pity so many people think poorly of themselves because how we see ourselves affects almost every aspect of our life. This image of ourselves is called the self-image or the self-concept.

Remember, in the last chapter we discussed how to reframe a situation to see it better; now we will consider reframing the way we see ourselves. To do this we will examine how self-concept is formed, how it develops and how we can change it. If you can master this, and it's not difficult, your success is guaranteed.

Our self-concept begins to take shape as soon as we are born and, sadly, for most of us it is a downhill cycle. We are born with a brain that is more powerful than the world's best computer but, like a computer, our brain has to be programmed. We are not born with instruction books tied around our waists so "most people" go through life accepting whatever programs society wants to give them. Because we live in a world that is basically negative, most of the programs are negative too. This trial and error method of programming the brain with whatever happens to come along takes its inevitable toll and as a result some people go through life oblivious to what they might have become if they had only followed some simple rules.

Think of your brain as a blank memory chip that is continually bombarded with messages from the day of your birth. These are stored till the day you die and your brain reacts to every situation in the light of what is stored in memory.

To help you understand self-concept, think about an imaginary person we'll call Ms X. She just happened to be born with a tall, strong body into a household where the family tended to be big eaters and ate a lot of junk food. Naturally she copied this pattern and developed the same eating habits as the rest of the family; her brain had been programmed since birth that this was a normal diet. Because of her naturally solid build and her bad eating habits she became quite plump.

Her mother, Mrs X, was also plump from the same combination of a naturally large frame and bad diet, but she always desired to have a figure like the slim models featured in all the magazines. She was forever going on crash diets to try to look like these so-called glamorous people but the diets only lasted a short while and she was back on the junk food path again. Ms X often heard her mother say, "I've got no willpower — I just can't stick with anything." Mr and Mrs X often had violent arguments, particularly when he had been drinking too much, and Ms X would hear her father call her mother names like "fat", "ugly" and "stupid".

Ms X's brain was soon programmed with the beliefs that slim was better than plump, being overweight meant you were ugly as well as stupid, anybody from her family was doomed to be overweight, and furthermore they had no willpower. It got worse. Ms X's schoolmates teased her about being overweight and by the time she was 14 years old she regarded herself as a total loser — fat, ugly and stupid. That was her self-concept.

Contrast the case of Ms Y who was born with the same build in similar economic circumstances. Her parents knew the importance of a good diet and exercise and taught her from an early age that she was lucky to have such a strong, healthy body and that she should take care of it. The parents praised her qualities and never made derogatory comments about each other in front of her. From the day she was born she was treated as a special person by her parents and taught that, although life had its ups and downs, she was smart enough to handle whatever life dished up to her.

Ms X and Ms Y were almost identical on the day they were born but by the time they turned 14, their belief in themselves was radically different. Why? Solely because of the way their brains had been programmed since birth. Their behaviour matched their individual self-concepts. Ms X saw each problem as further proof of her stupidity. Ms Y saw problems as a challenge and an opportunity to learn. Ms X reached a stage where she felt there was no point in trying because anything she did try was certain to fail. Failure was her program.

You will read more about self-concept in a later chapter about positive mental attitude but the above example should help you to know how self-concept develops. The input from the world around you programs your brain and you start to act in accordance with those programs. These actions are in line with that programming and therefore reinforce it.

We develop our self-concept mainly by what we tell ourselves, by what others say to us and from situations we observe and take part in. Napoleon Hill tells how he regarded himself at age nine as a criminal in the making because his father had always treated him like one. Luckily his father remarried a great woman who reversed all the damage his father had done. When Dad introduced the young Napoleon as "the meanest boy in Wise County", she replied, "You are wrong...he is a very alert and intelligent boy and all he needs is some worthy objective toward which to direct his very good mind."

That was the turning point in Napoleon Hill's life — when, at the age of nine, he received his first compliment.

To further illustrate the point, we will tell you something about Noel's life, because in his experience it is the illusions of life that play a major role in fouling up our self-concept.

Noel says...

My father was a pig farm manager so naturally I was the "pig farmer's son". My brother and I were never short of love or food but there was very little spare money.

Because I went to a small country school, there weren't too many opportunities to play much sport and my spare time was spent helping around the farm. When I got to high school I discovered that all those who had already been playing sport for their school went into the sports team and those of us who were left over were given a softball bat and left to amuse ourselves. This immediately produced two types of people in my mind: "sporting stars" who were in the school team with big badges on their pockets and "the non-sporting types" who had no sporting ability.

By the age of 14 I had a self-concept of being the pig farmer's son who was too clumsy to play sport. It's an awful feeling to be the last one picked when the sides are being chosen.

I found my escape in books but the problem with the books I read is that they all starred the superhero that deep down I wanted to be. It's bad enough to feel you're a person with no sporting ability from a deprived background, but once you start comparing yourself with all the heroes in the novels you are in real trouble. I did not know then that comparing yourself with others is one of the silliest things you can do.

My parents were ardent Royalists which meant my parents strongly believed in a class system where the classes didn't mix. Apparently, we were on the middle rungs and, for my own sake, it was drummed into me that people from our end of the ladder shouldn't try to climb up it much further. If we did try, the unavoidable outcome of trying to rise above our station would be frustration and disappointment. Luckily, they also programmed me that people from our station were "good honest workers". That bit of mind programming has stood me in good stead until this day.

We don't know where you're at right now and we don't know the background you come from. However, it is almost certain that you have suffered your fair share of negative programming. Your parents might have split up and you could still be feeling the effects of it; maybe you've suffered abuse or have been bullied or teased. Perhaps you trusted somebody who took advantage of you. Almost certainly you have suffered the insecurity of adolescence.

Actor Michael Caine described his teenage years like this: "My nose was too big. The thinner you got the bigger it looked...these problems all sound insignificant to adults, but to teenagers they take on an almost suicidal importance. Teenage children spend a ridiculous amount of time looking in the mirror as their facial structure convulses, rises and sinks like a pot of boiling porridge.

When all this is covered with a strategically placed veneer of pimples, you have the reason why most children never smile between the ages of 13 and 19. It is a terrible period for most kids."

Adjusting your self-concept

Self-concept does not develop overnight nor can you change it overnight. What you **can** do is start to make changes slowly and eventually the results will show. The following ideas will help you do it.

(1) Be aware that self-concept does exist and that yours has been programmed since birth. This awareness will help you start to change it.

(2) Don't become angry about the negative programming you have received so far or start blaming other people for doing it to you. You cannot change what has passed and you are wasting time by dwelling on it. Everybody who has affected you was, in turn, affected by somebody else and it is as unfair to blame them for their actions as it is for somebody to blame you for yours. You will spend the rest of your life in the future, which is where you should be concentrating your efforts.

(3) Be thankful for some of that negative programming because it may be a source of motivation for you. Some psychologists have referred to your negative

experiences as the "burr under the saddle" that spurs people on to success. Frank Sinatra said, "The best revenge is massive success", and you can act on that by reframing your negative experiences with the words "I'll show them". Remember, opposition is a help not a hindrance. Kites rise against the wind, not with it.

In 1964, after campaigning for racial equality, a South African man was given a life sentence and thrown in prison to rot. Rather than giving up, he began studying Afrikaans with the hope of building mutual respect with his captors and converting them to his cause. Twenty-seven years later, Nelson Mandela was released from prison. After his impassioned pleas for equality caught hearts and minds around the world, he was elected President of South Africa—the first non-white head of state in the country's history. Reflecting on his extraordinary life, he famously said: "I never lose. I win or I learn."

UFC champion Conor McGregor used a similar mantra throughout his career. Early on, when his record stood at a hardly threatening four wins and two losses, he refused to let the setbacks define him. Instead, McGregor continued to hone his skills and apply what he learned. An eight-fight win streak caught the eye of Dana White and the Irishman was signed to the UFC. A few short years after, he defeated José Aldo, one of the greatest fighters of all time, in 13 seconds—the fastest finish in UFC title fight history. The following year, his coach John Kavanagh released a book documenting the extraordinary journey with his star pupil entitled *Win or Learn*, echoing Mandela's fortitude. Today, Conor McGregor is one of the most recognised athletes on the planet.

(4) Understand that your self-concept develops from what goes into your brain. Therefore, take great care to prevent any more negative programs taking hold. You probably haven't realised the main input to your brain is "self-talk" which is what you say to yourself continually. A good example is what people say when they are playing sport. You'll hear statements like "My passing sucks today" or "My backhand is no good" or "I'm kicking like crap".

If you want to prove to yourself how self-concept works, reinforce the other person's concept by saying, "Yes — it's a pity, isn't it?" and watch what happens. We guarantee they'll get even worse. You could then try to help them improve by praising their good shots. Depending on the sport you prefer, read one of the Timothy Gallwey Inner Game books that show you how to excel through the use of mental techniques.

Gallwey states: "It was pointed out that the desire for improvement is natural, that man has a unique tendency to interfere with his own development, and that the primary form of interference is the forming of limiting images about himself and of trying to prove his own worth...Why are we so eager to accept beliefs about who we are, to identify with our performance appearance and roles?"

Exploring these ideas through books will help you to become more conscious of the way your self-concept affects every action you take.

(5) Resolve that you will never again say anything negative about yourself. There is almost a tradition that we play down our achievements, but we have never heard any of the real winners we know knocking themselves. If somebody pays you a compliment, accept it with a simple "thank you" and don't feel the need to add something derogatory about yourself to show how humble you are.

(6) Start going out of your way to help self-concept of other people by giving them praise and encouragement and never knocking them. Nothing will improve your own self-concept like helping the self-concept of others.

Noel says...

Never underestimate the power of your words on other people. I had words said to me when I was a teenager that still hurt today even though they were said more in fun than malice. Conversely I owe much of my success to encouraging words. I vividly remember when a fairly prominent member of the community I lived in said to me, "I've been watching you. You will go a long way". I was

40 when that happened and the words came at a time when I was going through a time of great self-doubt and inner conflict. Few experiences have given me such a boost.

(7) Establish a pattern of small successes and build on them. You will only harm your self-concept if, after reading this book, you set yourself huge impossible goals and then fail to achieve them. Our aim is to get you thinking like a person who can solve problems and overcome difficulties. Every small success you can notch up will give you the strength to go for a larger one.

For example, say your goal was to run a marathon. The last thing you should do is feel the burst of excitement and try running a marathon right away. You will quickly be injured, or worse. A better strategy is to channel that excitement into planning—perhaps you could find a coach to give you a program that incrementally gets you to your goal, a dietitian to get your nutrition on track, a pair of running shoes designed for long distance running, and a training partner so you can hold each other accountable. Equipped with the right ingredients, you could hit your target in the quickest possible time while mitigating the chance of failure. Consistency is king, and the right plan facilitates it.

(8) Read as many autobiographies as you can. By doing this you will have the privilege of sharing the thoughts of achievers. You will discover they had exactly the same doubts, fears and bad programming as you have experienced.

Hollywood legend Arnold Schwarzenegger was born in Austria, a country not known for its film stars. As a teenager, he set his sights on becoming the greatest bodybuilder who ever lived. At the age of 20, after becoming the youngest ever winner of the Mr Universe title, he turned his attention to acting. Arnold said: "I wanted to be a film star. Everyone told me, "It can't be done. You've got this huge, monstrous body, you're overly developed and you've got a strange accent — it doesn't fit into the movies." But I didn't listen because that was **their** rules. I was convinced I could do it. Then I got a big break in *Conan the Barbarian*. And there the director said, "If we didn't have Schwarzenegger, we would have to build one". Then when I did *The Terminato*r, the line "I'll be back" became one of the most famous lines in movie history, all because of my crazy accent. It just shows that you never listen if someone says you can't do something.

If I had listened to the naysayers, I would still be in the Austrian Alps yodelling. Anything I've ever attempted, I was always willing to fail. Work your butt off, and leave no stone unturned. Trust yourself no matter what anyone else thinks. Believe in yourself and your vision, and success will come."

When you read statements like this you will appreciate how your own progress is being held back by illusions.

James says...

Some years ago I was fortunate enough to meet a well known business consultant, author and public speaker Sergio Carlo Maresca over a coffee. We spoke about what we'd done recently and what each other had planned for the future in regards to both career and personal development. I was immediately impressed by his forward and honest insights on life.

I was at somewhat of a crossroads and he enquired as to what I was interested in pursuing for the future. I mentioned a strong desire to get into public speaking, but at that point lacked the direction to do so.

He said I'd be a fantastic speaker and promised to recommend me for a speaking engagement almost a year away. I agreed, half expecting to never hear anything again. Ten months later, I was contacted regarding an event and ended up speaking in front of 700 people. Although terrified backstage beforehand, it remains one of the most rewarding experiences of my life — and it never would've have happened if it wasn't for his inspiration and encouragement.

There's a lot of content available available to help re-program your brain. The message of this chapter is that it is highly likely that you have a low self-esteem because of the bad programming your brain has received up to this point. When you have finished this book you will be well on the way to installing good new programs, which will replace the old ones that may be holding you back now. At this stage it's enough that you be aware of the extraordinary influence of self-concept.

Remember, the most important opinion is how you feel about yourself. If you're struggling with your place in the world, you might be interested in James' online program *Win the Day Accelerator* that focuses heavily on developing self-awareness, living in alignment with your highest values, and creating a life of freedom.

Key points:

- We develop our self-concept mainly by what we tell ourselves, by what others say to us and from situations we observe and take part in.

- You cannot change what has passed and you are wasting time by dwelling on it.

- Never again say anything negative about yourself.

- Nothing will improve your own self-concept like helping the self-concept of others.

- Every small success you can notch up will give you the strength to go for a larger one.

- Read as many autobiographies as you can so you can share the thoughts of high achievers.

8

What you give is what you get

or

The law of sowing and reaping

There are 10 weaknesses against which most of us must guard ourselves. One of these is the habit of trying to reap before we have sown and the other nine are all wrapped up in the one practice of creating alibis to cover every mistake made.

Napoleon Hill

The message of this chapter is simple — we can only get out of life what we put into it.

> **James says...** 🗨
>
> *We all fight our own internal battles. Throughout high school and university, I privately went through some extremely debilitating struggles with anxiety. I felt a deep sense of shame, having been born in a prosperous country like Australia, being fortunate enough to have a good education, and raised in a lov-*

ing family; yet, pondering these advantages only made the situation ten times worse. Many times I felt completely hopeless, like a malfunctioned human destined for the scrapheap, while I saw everyone else seemingly have the perfect life.

Many years after permanently defeating what had been such a horrible burden, I was approached by Success Magazine, *a publication I had been an avid reader of for years. They asked me to contribute an article to their Summer 2019 issue, which freaked me out because I thought, "Who would be interested in my story? What would I even say!?"*

Something told me that was the appropriate time and avenue to reveal the private battle that previously had only been known to a few people. Writing it was therapeutic, but the process of releasing it out into the world was extremely liberating. Success *loved it so much they gave it four pages, and today I still get emails from people who mention they had been through, or are still in, a similar battle, and just want to thank me for raising awareness and trying to help.*

Now, I understand that all of us—literally every single one of us—has an amazing story, but we're so conditioned by the bad seeds inside of us or worrying about what other people might think that we diminish just how significant we can be. Unfortunately, many people succumb to the darkness and never get to see what magnificent light they could have shared with the world, which was the primary motivator for Noel and I to write a book such as this one.

Irrespective of where you're at now, or what adversity you face in the future, everything you need to succeed will still be in your possession. In fact, that adversity, no matter how tough, might just end up being your greatest asset—or, at the very least, a springboard to extraordinary achievement. In Think and Grow Rich: The Legacy, *you can see dozens of stories of people who have been hit by cars, gone blind as a teenager, overcome long-term drug addiction, and pretty much anything else you can think of, to make their mark on the world. You can too.*

Just remember to keep planting the good seeds, no matter how bad things seem.

Don't we human beings have strange thinking habits? We would never sit in front of an empty fireplace hoping, by some miracle, that heat would come out it. We know if we wanted heat we would find some dry wood, build the fire and then strike a match. Yet we are often guilty of hoping for many things in life to happen before we take the necessary steps to bring about the desired outcome. It's called trying to reap the harvest before we have sown the seeds.

Haven't you wanted top grades without doing the work, sporting honours without doing the practice, a fit body without doing the exercise? Of course you have — that's human nature. No wonder the exercise machines on late-night infomercials that promise an amazing body and six-pack abs for five minutes work are so popular. Ray Kroc, the founder of McDonald's, tells the story of a famous musician who was accosted by one of those chatty society women at a cocktail party. "I'd give anything to play like you," she said. "No, you wouldn't" was the reply, "You wouldn't be prepared to practise for hours, to give up the social life, to exist on a pittance while you were trying to make your mark—that is what made the difference."

The good news for you is that "most people" spend all their life wishing for things they haven't earned and only a few, that's right about 10%, make the effort to get them.

Every Saturday night millions of people sit round their televisions waiting for their "numbers" to come up. Of course, as weeks pass and no one wins the jackpot, the prize gets bigger and attracts more media attention. One of the most publicised wins was that of an American who bought a lotto ticket at a tiny store in downtown Los Angeles on 19 July 2023 and who is more than $1.6 billion richer after winning the Powerball jackpot. It is the sixth largest win in US history and the third largest in the game's history. It's exciting news, but don't set your hopes on winning it—the game's abysmal odds of 1 in 292.2 million are designed to build big prizes that draw more players. Your future is too precious to leave at the whim of such ridiculous odds.

There are two rules you need to know about sowing and reaping. The obvious one is:

(1) You cannot reap before you have sown.

The less obvious one is:

(2) You always reap far more than you sow.

Nature is clever. She knows it would be a waste of your time to plant a cup of corn if all you got back at harvest time was another cup of corn. No, plant a cup of corn and you may well get back bags and bags of corn. Better still, if you ate some of the corn and planted the rest, those bags of corn seed you plant have the potential to produce thousands upon thousands of bags of corn.

In *Making Money Made Simple*, in the chapter titled "The Torch", Noel tells the story of a poor boy Orison Marden who found out about the secrets of success in 1870 by reading *Self Help* by Samuel Smiles. Marden became the founder of *Success Magazine* and Napoleon Hill was one of his first reporters. Hill then wrote *Think and Grow Rich* which has been read by millions of people and inspired the likes of W. Clement Stone, Jim Rohn and Og Mandino. Literally millions of people have been helped to a better life because the writings of Samuel Smiles sowed one tiny seed in the brain of Orison Marden.

Unfortunately the law of sowing and reaping works in both the positive and the negative. If you sow a few weed seeds, you end up with a huge crop of weeds. Therefore the more "good" seeds you sow, the more "good" results you harvest and the more "bad" seeds you sow, the more "bad" results you have to cope with. What happens if you don't sow anything? It will be more weeds, not corn, that will pop up.

Examples of this are the people who drop out of high school because the work is tough, and then try to find jobs to bring in some money, and then make no effort to improve their skills. They attract a paltry harvest. As a result of never gaining worthwhile skills, they spend their whole lives in lowly paid jobs or living on welfare. Thus, they cheat themselves out of millions of dollars of extra money they could have earned if they had made the effort to improve their knowledge.

You must also be vigilant in protecting what you sow. There will be many things that try to impede your road to wealth — "most people" would rather have you on their level so they can feel better about themselves. But ask yourself "What seeds am I planting if I give into these external forces?" Just as a farmer uses scarecrows, pesticides and immense care when tending the harvest, you must apply the same dedication and foresight to avoid the negative pull of those around you. Your rewards will be far greater for doing so.

When Noel was working in the bank a teller "borrowed" a few dollars from the cash drawer. He was found out and the bank administration ordered his instant dismissal. It was only a small amount of money, and he had intended to put it back next day, but it cost him a promising career.

What excites us about sowing and reaping is the way small seeds can grow and the way a seed planted now can produce a crop many years later, often when you least expect it. This is why it is important to keep sowing "good" seeds all the time, for you never know when they will suddenly burst forth into a crop.

Noel says...

I made a speech several years ago to a group of car dealers and their staff. A new car salesman named Roy approached me and handed me his business card with the words, "When you want to buy a new car give me a ring". I took one look at the card and noticed that he worked for a dealership that was 50 kilometres away. When I told him I always bought locally he smiled and said, "When you have experienced my service you will buy from me". Some feeling inside me made me keep the card and six months later I was shopping for a car. I tried the local dealership but was put off by a rude salesman who told me an obvious lie by trying to pass off last year's model as a current one. That's one of the traps of buying a car in January — that difference of one month means a big difference when you come to sell it.

Shortly after, I phoned Roy. He sold me a car and has been looking after my cars since. Servicing is not a problem because he always has my car collected from home and provides a loan car for the day. I have referred many other people to him and I am sure they, in turn, have referred others. The act of handing me a business card (and, in doing so, sowing a single tiny seed) has given Roy a harvest of over 100 sales.

We could fill this book with stories like the ones above but we are sure you have got the message. Now you should ask yourself what good and bad seeds you are sowing and remember that many bad seeds take a long time to surface.

Many older people now have problems with scores of tiny skin cancers that keep popping up on their faces and bodies because they spent too much time in the sun without protection when they were young. Thousands of people die every year as a result of slowly destroying their lungs with vaping or cigarette smoke. Most people reach retirement age without enough money to live on because they never "got around" to starting an investment program until it was too late.

You are young and have the opportunity to start planting seeds now that will provide a harvest beyond your expectations. In the next chapter we'll teach you how to do it.

 Key points:

- We can only get out of life what we put into it.
- Ask yourself what good and bad seeds you are sowing.
- Be vigilant in protecting what you sow.
- It's never too early to plant seeds that will change your life.

9

Goals —
What you set is
what you get

Setting goals is the first step in
turning the invisible into the visible.
Anthony Robbins

The message in this chapter is that the most extraordinary things start to happen when you set goals.

Noel says...

One day at a conference I bumped into Kevin Carton who was then the Australian head of the Sheraton Hotel chain. Kevin is not just a successful executive, he was also an Olympic hockey champion. I asked him the secret of his success. Guess what the answer was? "Setting goals, plus the ability to keep a smile on my face when the game got tough — that really used to bug the opponents."

We have spent thousands of hours reading books and listening to interviews about success and have found there is one factor on which they all agree. That, is the importance of setting goals — the ability to decide what you want and then make a detailed plan to go after it. If you can master the art of doing that your success is guaranteed, for you have literally given yourself the power to design your own future.

When you set a goal you make a statement about something you wish to happen. However, a properly set goal is much stronger than a wish, it's a commitment. Contrast this to the everyday chatter of most people: "I wish I was happy", "I wish I could stop work", " I wish I could travel". These are not goals; they are dreams that will probably never happen. There is nothing wrong with dreaming, but far too many resign themselves to the dream when, with a little effort, they could have had the real thing.

The moment you commit to a goal, strange forces come into play and incredible things start to happen around you. It seems that once you set a goal your brain works on it day and night, even when you are sleeping, working out ways to bring it about and attracting events and people to you that will help make it happen.

James says...

I once had the opportunity to interview poker legend Daniel Negreanu to learn more about his secrets to success. Negreanu mentioned that he creates a "vision board", a collection of motivational images and statements of intent that guide him toward his goals for that year; this helps him tap into the power within, progress on what is most important, and ultimately become the best version of himself.

During our interview I asked him, "What is the secret to bringing your A-game every time you sit down at a table?" He replied, "I think the secret is to focus on what my intention is. I believe in sitting down and saying to yourself "What is your goal?" A lot of people just play and they're not even thinking about what they're actually doing there. So for me, my intention is clear—it's to win. But aside from that, it's most important to me to have fun because when I'm having fun, success comes." He knows what he needs for the best performance, and then sets a goal to make it happen.

You can set goals in many areas of your life. Your goal may be to buy a car, have a holiday in Europe, lose six kilos in weight, buy a house, pay off a debt, win the local tennis championship, get a promotion at work or complete a study course.

It works like this every time: you desire an outcome, to reach it takes some effort on your part, and you will have to give up something to get it. If you are saving for a car, house or holiday, it involves taking money from each pay packet and putting it aside. You have to give up the fun of spending now so you can achieve your goal. It's been called the ice cream/bicycle syndrome. You forgo eating the ice cream today so you can have a bicycle tomorrow.

Similarly you must devote time to exercise and healthy eating to lose weight, and put in many hours of practice or study if you wish to win the tennis match or complete the study course. There is always something to give up. Notice how it all gets back to the law of sowing and reaping. Those who do not want to pay the price of giving up in order to get, finish with nothing.

Setting goals

We'll now take you through the steps of setting a goal. We'll use the example of having a goal to buy a car.

(1) First you must clearly define exactly what you want. The brain cannot act on a vague goal such as "I want to own a car".

You must have a clear picture in your mind of what the car will look like. This includes make, model, colour, number of doors, features, etc. Find that car's brochure either from a car dealership or through an internet search, and make sure it has at least one coloured photograph of the car. Then stick it up on your bedroom wall where it will be the first and last thing you see each day. If you are choosing a second-hand car you should be able to print a description and photos from one of the many car websites.

Next go to the local car dealership and have one of the staff take a photo of you sitting in the car of your dreams. Make sure it is the same model and colour as the one you want.

(2) Name the date on which it is to happen. It is no good saying, "I want to buy a car". That's another wish. You must say something like "By 20 January 20XX I will own a white Toyota Model XXX."

(3) Draw up a plan to get it. Suppose the desired date is 24 months away, the cost of the car is $15,000 and you have $8,200 saved up now. The difference is $6,800 and you have 24 months to find it. Therefore you need to save $280 a month. Can you do that? To find out, you'll have to draw up a budget — this is covered in chapter 19.

What happens if you do all the figures but the plan does not seem possible in the time frame you have set? For example, you list your income and all your expenses and decide there is no way you can save the $280 a month you need. Now you have reached the interesting part—you must stretch your mind to try to find ways to achieve the goal. Ask yourself if the goal is realistic, even though it's a bit of a challenge. If it is realistic you will have to think of ways to find the extra money. If that's not practical you will have to modify your goals.

Let's imagine it is realistic but you just don't have that $280 a month available. It's then a matter of cutting your spending or earning more money. Go over your budget and see what you can prune out of it. Are you buying lunches when you could be taking them from home? Could you get a lift to work instead of using public transport? Can you cut down on clothes?

Now think about ways to increase your income. Is a second job possible? Can you get a job at the car dealership washing cars and have the payment taken off the car price? Do the neighbours need somebody to mow their lawn or to babysit their children?

The best part about learning how to set goals is the change that takes place in you as a human being. Once you think about achieving your goals you start to focus on ways to solve problems. This is in stark contrast to "most people" who spend their life talking about the problems and never get around to finding any solutions. By concentrating on the solutions instead of the problems you distance yourself from the herd.

You have now started to become a human being who has the ability to set goals, to make plans to achieve them and to adjust those plans if circumstances change. In other words you are starting to take control of your life. Congratulations, you are well on the road to success. If you're ready to start setting goals that work, download the *Success Plan Template* that James uses with all his clients.[2]

Why goal setting works

Goal setting works for this reason:

- Setting goals gives your mind a focus. Think about what happens when your goal is to save for a car, you need $280 a month to do it and the photo of the car is on your wall as well as in your wallet. Sure, you may be tempted to break out and waste some money but you will clearly understand that by having the "ice cream" now you will delay "riding the bicycle". You will also find the goal of owning the "bicycle" will become so dominant that the wish for the "ice cream" will be far easier to fight.

If you have neglected an assignment and abruptly found the deadline approaching, you would have experienced the power that comes from goal setting. Suddenly working on

---

[2] Go to *https://jameswhitt.com/go-time* to download your free *Success Plan Template*.

that project takes over your thoughts and you find a power and concentration you never experienced until the deadline drew near. You become focused on the task to the exclusion of all other thoughts. This is what goal setting is all about.

Competing goals?

The problem with setting goals is that you can become trapped among competing interests. You may want to buy a car, have a holiday, buy a house, a new outfit, party with your friends, enrol in a study course and win the sporting event. What do you do?

Noel says...

The solution is to try to put together a list of goals that will work together. For example, when I was studying accounting after I was married, I studied from 7pm to 11pm from Monday through to Thursday. This gave me Friday night and the weekend for other activities. Each study night I went for a 30-minute jog at 9pm and followed it with a quick shower. This accounted for the exercise goal but it also gave me a bonus. The run and shower halfway through my study freshened me up for the rest of the night.

I also got a dose of motivation because I always jogged along the same route. Every night I would pass a house and notice the owner sitting in the same chair watching television. I told myself, "In four years I'll have my degree and he'll still be sitting in the same spot wasting his life."

James says... 💬

When I was 19 I was saving for an overseas holiday, but was spending too much money out with friends on weekends. My savings were being eaten away by my social life. I then began working in a nightclub on most Friday and Saturday nights doing bartending. After a few weeks I was amazed at how much my savings had grown. Rather than spending $100 out with my friends, I was actually earning the $100 and was able to put it straight into the holiday savings.

Maybe it's time to think outside the box a little. For example, if you combine a savings goal with the goal of completing a study course, you could opt to stay home and complete a minimum of three hours study five nights a week. Although you'll likely miss out on social events from time to time, you can put the money away that you would have spent, and you'll be able to dedicate much more time to the course, with both actions accelerating your journey to the life you want. Looking back, you won't regret the social occasions you missed, and it may even strengthen your relationships with your closest friends because you'll value your time with them more.

Remember to keep a balance in your life, so don't neglect going out and having fun with your friends; just do it sensibly and in ways that align with your goals. As you can see from the above examples, managing your time more efficiently can help more than you ever imagined.

Start with small goals

This book is all about helping you to make minor changes in your life that will lead to bigger changes later. Because you improve your self-concept through a series of little successes, it is best to start your goal-setting program with small goals that have a strong chance of achievement. Once you have mastered these you can move onto bigger ones.

For example, if you have several small debts you may set a goal to pay one of them off quickly, say, in three months. Perhaps there is a piece of sports equipment you want, like a pair of running shoes. Set yourself the goal of saving up for it. Just practise the techniques we showed you of writing it down, stating a time for realisation of the goal, and focusing your mind on it.

While you are doing this, remember that goal setting is useless unless you take the right actions to achieve them.

There is no point in setting a goal to buy a car in 18 months if you continue to spend all your money on shopping and entertainment; you are fooling yourself if your goal is to lose weight yet you still snack on pastries and soft drink. Ask yourself "Does my behaviour match my goals?" If the answer is "no", you had better do some quiet thinking about where you really want to go in life.

Don't be frightened to use tricks to help you stay on track.

For example:

- Exercise with a friend. This will make you turn up at the right time, you can motivate each other to do better, and you may even compete against each other to see who gets the best results.

- Leave your credit cards at home. This will stop the impulse buy and keep you focused on your needs rather than your wants.

- Only do your grocery shopping *after* a meal. This will keep you from buying junk food and other unnecessary items.

When writing a book we usually arrange the publication date first to provide us with a firm deadline to finish. Otherwise we fall into to the "We'll start next week" trap, shuffle papers for months and never get around to doing anything of substance.

The salami technique

A variation of starting with small goals is to use the "salami technique" which gets its name because it is like slicing thin strips off a piece of sausage. You simply figure out what your goal is and then break it down into a series of smaller sub goals. Then each sub goal becomes a series of more realistic and achievable goals that, when achieved, equates to the original larger goal.

We use this technique when we're writing a book because a book, like accumulating a million dollars, is far too big a goal to grasp. It is much easier to first make a list of the chapter headings and then work on the sub goals of writing each chapter.

James says...

Courses on "how to write" often encourage you to come up with the topic sentence of each paragraph, then several supporting points, then a concluding sentence — there's your paragraph. Writing a number of topic sentences and paragraphs sounds much less daunting than a 2,000-word essay.

Famous Chinese military strategist Sun Tzu literally wrote the book on the relationship between strategy (broader goals) and tactics (how to achieve them). In his timeless classic "The Art of War", one of his defining messages was "Strategy without tactics is the slowest route to victory. Tactics without strategy is the noise before defeat." Each night before you go to bed, write down 3–5 tasks that you must do the following day to achieve your goals. Put them on your phone or notebook or some other place you'll see them regularly. The key is — don't go to bed until they're completed. With a daily plan to achieve all that you desire, your chances of victory increase exponentially.

In *Making Money Made Simple* Noel gives the example of the 10-step ladder to a million dollars. The ladder is only 10 steps and the first step is to save a mere $2,000. "Most people" take one look at the million dollars at the top of the ladder, decide it's all too difficult and go back to watching television. The smart ones know you can only climb a ladder one step at a time and focus on the $2,000. When they have climbed that rung they move to the next goal, which is to accumulate $4,000. That is also easy because it's only a matter of putting together another $2,000, which they now know they can do.

It is in our nature to be encouraged when we complete a task and to be discouraged when we fail to complete a task. By working on many small sub goals that combine into a large goal we manage to keep up our enthusiasm as well as finally accomplishing great things.

You now know what goal setting is and why it works. Some of the books listed at the back will give you more information. We'll now move onto three essential skills that will speed you on your journey to success.

Key points:

- The common thread in all success stories is the importance of setting goals.
- Live your goal by putting tangible reminders in the areas where you spend the most time.
- Make your goal as specific as possible.
- By concentrating on the solutions instead of the problems you distance yourself from the herd.
- Start with small goals. Making minor changes now will lead to bigger changes later.
- Use tricks to keep you on track, like exercising with a friend.
- Adopt the salami technique — break a big goal down into a series of smaller ones.
- Make sure your behaviour matches your goals.

10

The three essential skills

*Do a little more than average and from
that point on your progress multiplies
itself out of all proportion to the efforts put in.*
Paul J. Meyer

You will get out of life whatever you put into it — good
and bad. This chapter focuses on three skills that will
help you into a leadership role, for it is through leadership
that you can increase your opportunities.

Our aim is to help you become a person who is in charge
of your life and who can make things happen instead of
being at the mercy of other people's whims. As Jim Rohn
said, "Either you are making plans or somebody is making
plans for you." Therefore you should cultivate those habits that will transform you into a leader instead of a fol-
lower. Leaders are paid more, have more opportunities for
self-development and there are more openings available
to them.

There are three special attributes that will help you become a leader. None of them are particularly difficult, they don't need any special aptitudes and they are available to almost everybody. The big plus is that you can pick up these skills quickly and, when you master them, they will probably make a great difference to your life in a short time.

The three attributes in leadership development are:

(1) Get into the habit of going the extra mile.

(2) Acquire some basic sales skills.

(3) Learn to speak well in public.

As you can see, there is nothing too hard about any of them. The first is a habit that you should be able to pick up in a month, and the other two are skills that are easily learned. Just don't underestimate the way they can change your life and, as you read this chapter, remember that "most people" never attain them. Consequently, anybody who makes the effort to master them automatically goes to the head of the field.

Going the extra mile

Noel says...

Some years ago, my wife and I were driving home from the annual speech night of my old school — Salisbury State High School, and we were pondering over the way fate had worked in that time. It had been many years since my first speech night at the school and I had returned to present the prizes and make a speech. I doubt if anybody in my school would have dreamed that many years later I would have been on the stage giving out the prizes but, against all expectations, it had happened. We tried to focus on what I had done right, as opposed to the hundreds of things I had done wrong, and discovered two factors that I am sure helped me along the way. They were going the extra mile and being a non-stop learner.

My parents had instilled in me how important it was to always give of my best and it had always seemed sensible to me to keep learning and discovering new things. However, it wasn't until I read Think and Grow Rich *that I discovered that going the extra mile has always been the hallmark of successful people.*

Consider the following incident. It is not earth shattering, yet it has stuck in my mind since the day it happened and I have recounted it to audiences around the world.

The time was 7.50am on a Tuesday, and I was staying at the Sheraton Hotel in Townsville. I was heading down to breakfast and was keen to pick up a copy of the Cairns Post *newspaper because I knew it would contain a photo and an article about a speech I made there the day before. I said to the bellboy, "Where is the paper shop? I am after a copy of the* Cairns Post.*" He told me the papers were sold from the small store in the lobby but it did not open till 8am. "No problem," I replied, "I'll pick one up after breakfast."*

I went to breakfast and promptly forgot all about it until 8.05am when the bell boy appeared at my table with a newspaper. "Here's your Cairns Post,*" he said and disappeared. Now that's what I call going the extra mile.*

Later I reported the incident to Elin Power who was the training manager of the Sheraton at the time and she told me the staff had been trained to try to second-guess what the guests wanted and to surprise them in just the way the bell boy had surprised me. Was that a big deal or not? It was only a small action and anybody could have done it. Yes, it was a big deal, it is memorable and it causes a ripple whenever I mention it to an audience. That is because it was so unusual!

Contrast this to the case of a 16-year-old girl who came to our office to do some temporary work. She was after a permanent job and, unbeknown to her, we were looking for a permanent junior. She was a good worker and would have been offered the job except for one bad habit. Every afternoon at 4.55pm she was packed up and waiting to leave. That is the opposite of going the extra mile. She was never offered the job.

> *A friend of mine is an executive of a large company. He says, "When we are hiring staff we look for the person who has done a lot of extracurricular activities while they were at school. We don't want somebody who thinks life is a 9 to 5 job."*

By going the extra mile you ensure you get noticed, which means you will usually be first in line for any special jobs that come along. These extra jobs give you the chance to learn more skills, to show more of your abilities to others and to move faster and faster along the road to wealth.

Acquiring sales skills

Unfortunately, far too many people have an image of "selling" as something cheap and nasty and regard salespeople as inferior beings who are not to be trusted. That's an unfortunate belief. Sure, there are some shonky hard-sell merchants about but most salespeople are honest and fill a vital role in our community. In most situations their role is to identify a problem, find the solution and convince the customers the solution is suitable for them.

Imagine you were considering a holiday. You would expect the sales consultant in the travel bureau to find out where you wished to go, work that in with what you wanted to spend and then plan an itinerary that would suit you and give you pleasure. If you are looking for a new outfit, the salesperson's job is to find something that you will feel good in, and in your price range.

In short, selling is the art of taking charge, knowing what to do and convincing others to take action. It requires similar skills to leadership. Top salespeople are among the highest paid people in the world because they are rare — few will put in the effort that is necessary to provide a high level of customer satisfaction.

There's another reason too. The pay of most salespeople is often directly related to their performance. That's right—they are paid according to the sales they make. Most people would find that too uncomfortable, but if you're serious about improving yourself, doesn't it make sense to be paid what you are worth? That way you can earn more than others if you are good enough.

If you think about it, nearly all highly paid jobs have an element of selling in them:

- A doctor selling a patient on the idea of giving up fast food.
- A coach convincing the team they can win.
- A professor selling the need for more funds for the department.
- A manager selling the employees on different work practices.
- A public relations expert selling the media on the idea of using a story.
- An author convincing a publisher to accept a book.

Even a parent selling their child on the idea of extra study would fit here. They all involve persuading another person towards a course of action that should be of benefit to that person.

Please don't confuse this with the idea of "hard sell" where indifferent or unscrupulous salespeople try to convince people to buy something that may be wrong for them just to make a sale. Yes, it does happen, but you will discover those people never seem to get far in life because they are ignoring some basic principles that will be revealed as you read further.

There is a vast array of books on selling online, and your local bookstore may also have books you can browse through. A simple internet search will allow you listen to a wide range of podcasts as well as listening to, and watching, some of the great salespeople of our time. See what you can find.

Developing sales skills will show you how to gain the trust of others, ask probing questions to get to the heart of a problem, handle troublemakers and persuade others to a course of action. These are all leadership skills that will point you to the top.

Learning to speak well in public

Do you know that most people would rather contract a serious disease than get on their feet and speak to an audience? Winston Churchill said, "The three most difficult things for a man to do are to climb a wall leaning away from you, to kiss a girl leaning away from you and to make an after-dinner speech." As a child, Churchill was painfully shy and stuttered but, through preparation, mastery of technique and practice, he became one of the greatest orators of the 20th century.

It's hard to understand this fear of public speaking because most children love to perform in public. Apparently at some point in our lives we become self-conscious and start being concerned about making a fool of ourselves.

There is a wealth of information about public speaking available, but to do it well you need experience, a sound knowledge of your subject and communication skills. These are not hard to acquire. Knowledge of your subject will come automatically as you continue studying your chosen field and you can gain experience while you are learning the communication skills.

The easiest way to start is to join an organisation like Toastmasters or Rostrum and become an active participant. Speak to established business leaders in your community, or someone you look up to, and ask for their recommendations. When you attend one of these clubs or gatherings, you will meet other frightened and no longer frightened people who are all learning to speak in front of a group.

Of course, you are likely to be terrified at first. But as American psychologist Susan Jeffers said, "Feel the fear and do it anyway."

You'll often find that standing up in front of people and starting your presentation is the hardest part. It's not very often that a person gets a few minutes into their speech and then gets nervous. Work on memorising the first 30 seconds of your speech and you're assured of a great start, which will get rid of any remaining fear in your body.

It's well worth the effort. As each speech passes you will feel more at ease. The time will then come when you look forward to standing up and holding forth. Then you will be able to help others overcome their fears as you develop your skills even further.

Once again, think outside the box. Does your job require interaction with customers? If so, your employer might be more than willing to fund some (or all) of the costs of a public speaking course, which will significantly improve your self-development.

Regard this moment as one of the many crossroads in your life — the road you take will have a vital bearing on where you finish. You can choose to think "I could never stand up and speak in public" and give in to your fears. This will make you even more scared to try anything new and may well deprive you of the chance to discover much of the potential you never knew you had. On the other hand, you may think, "I'll give it a go; I've got nothing to lose and everything to gain." Do this and you have just taken a big step on the road to success.

Think about it. We know that achievers do what "most people" are not prepared to do. If you make the effort to join a public speaking or debating group, you have faced a fear and overcome it. Furthermore, you have done something that most people are not prepared to do and have thus moved further down the path of self-development.

Remember — not trying guarantees failure; trying gives you a chance of success.

Key points:

- Through leadership you can increase your opportunities.
- Key steps in leader development are: getting into the habit of going the extra mile, acquiring some basic sales skills, and learning to speak well in public.
- Going the extra mile is the hallmark of successful people.
- Do something that most people are not prepared to do.
- Not trying guarantees failure; trying gives you a chance of success.

11

Finding your inner power

Everyone has inside them a piece of good news.
The good news is that you don't know how great
you can be, how much you can love, what you
can accomplish, and what your potential is!

Anne Frank

The message in this chapter is that you have many skills that you have not yet developed. If you develop your skills, you will expand the value of the service you can offer, which will increase your rewards in life.

> **Noel says...**
>
> *My life changed when I went to a breakfast to hear a talk by an American named Jim Rohn who we have mentioned several times in this book. I didn't want to go to the breakfast because at that stage in my life I foolishly thought I knew everything but something inside me drove me there. The theme of his lecture was "Don't wish it were easier — wish you were better". It really hit me.*

If you are like "most people", and like I was at the time, you have probably spent a lot of time wishing life was easier. You have almost certainly wished you did not have to cope with such ongoing problems as study, finding and keeping a job, money, and handling complex relationships with loved ones. That's a natural feeling. Unfortunately, you will find the problems don't vanish as you grow older — you just get a different set of problems. Hopefully by that time you'll have learned some of life's lessons and will be able to handle them a little better.

Listen to the conversations of those around you and notice that much of it is in the category of "I wish life was easier". It is full of complaining about problems and wishing that they would go away but, as no time is given to finding solutions, the situation seldom improves.

However, you now know about reframing and once you reframe your attitude from "wishing life was easier" to "wishing I was better" you can start to work on the skills that will make it better. When you do this you move the focus from worrying about problems to trying to find solutions. You can then start to take charge of your life instead of being a helpless victim in the control of others.

The solution to almost every problem is to educate yourself to handle it better. This process is called "self-development" and means that you make the time and effort to learn new skills. This will help you in several ways:

(1) New skills open up a new world of opportunities for you. These include job promotions, a chance to travel and the possibility of starting your own business.

Noel says...

When I read Think and Grow Rich *I set a goal to have my own business within 100 days. I was 34 and by this stage in my life I had experience in banking, conveyancing, personnel work, accounting, tax, property development and marketing. These all combined to make me a useful participant in a building business and within 130 days I was in partnership with a builder. He brought his building skills and experience to the venture and, combined, we were a highly effective team. The time I had spent in self-development paid off.*

(2) New skills boost your self-esteem. Because you feel better about yourself, you perform better. This makes you feel even better about yourself and you perform even better — so the cycle continues.

James says...

This is one of the most powerful things I have ever learned.

When you feel better about yourself, you share that joy and happiness with the world. If someone's having a rough day, a quick smile or a polite gesture on your behalf might be enough to turn it all around for them.

Develop the skill of being happy, and your inner power and positive energy will radiate to those around you. Once you practise this enough so that it happens automatically, you'll notice people are happy and confident around you. *And they will certainly enjoy your company because you have built your image as someone fun to be around.*

(3) Your improved skills enable you to render a better service. As your rewards in life will always match your service, it must follow that by improving your skills you improve your rewards in life.

(4) Opportunity favours the prepared. In every place of employment, from the factory to the opera, there will come a time when a key person becomes ill or unavailable, and then there is a frantic hunt for a replacement. If you are on the spot and have the skills, you are likely to get the chance to show your talents. Do the job well and you put yourself in line for promotion, which is another opportunity for you to learn even more skills.

(5) In this modern and fast-changing technological world you will fall behind your competitors if you fail to keep up to date. Continual self-development is one of the best ways to provide security because it ensures you are not being left behind.

A major enemy

Think about this one quickly "How much does a TV set cost to own?" You may guess a couple of hundred dollars a year, but we believe the figure is closer to $1,000 a month. That is the money you lose while you are wasting time watching it.

Distractions like television and social media are among your greatest enemies because they provide little by way of self-development yet offer continual temptation and distraction. The latest research tells us that teens spend an average of seven hours and 22 minutes on their phones a day – that's over 50 hours a week, or 2,600 hours a year. Just imagine where you would be if you spent even half of that on self-development?

In contrast, good books require some effort on your part and allow you to stop to think about the subject matter. They also allow you to re-read a passage if you wish.

James says...

Autobiographies can be a wonderful source of motivation, as well as one of the best ways to improve your mind, because they usually tell of the struggles and the feelings of inadequacy the authors went through. When we read this our own troubles fall into perspective and we can be inspired in the knowledge that other people have faced and overcome worse problems than we have had to endure.

While homeless, John Paul DeJoria used a $750 loan to launch a hair care company, John Paul Mitchell Systems, which now earns $1 billion in revenue each year. Sylvester Stallone wrote dozens of movie scripts, but no *one wanted to buy them. After selling his dog so he had enough money for food, Stallone wrote* Rocky *and stuck to his guns, only agreeing to sell the script if the studio cast him as the lead role in the film. The film went on to be nominated for 10 Academy Awards, with Best Actor and Best Original Screenplay nominations for Stallone. A penniless, depressed single mother J.K. Rowling had her manuscript rejected by 12 publishers; today the Harry Potter brand is estimated to be worth more than $25 billion. After reading about the struggles many people had to go through before they were successful, it seems futile to blame our troubles on mundane excuses or expect success to find us while we're sitting in front of the television.*

You should also think about effective learning, where you absorb material in the most efficient manner depending on what type of person you are. If you are a visual learner, try TED Talks, documentaries and educational magazines. If you crave a bit of peace and quiet, head to the nearest book store and see what you can find. If you are one of those people who find "there just aren't enough hours in the day", download audiobooks and podcasts to your mobile device so you can listen to them whenever you have a few minutes free.

When you find something you enjoy, share it with your most positive, ambitious and inspiring friends, and it won't be long before they return the favour and quality material heads your way without you needing to lift a finger.

Books have the power to change lives. The book *Self Help* by Samuel Smiles provided the motivation for Orison Marden to rise above his poor background, put himself through university and then start the publishing company that employed Napoleon Hill. The full story of the rise of Orison Marden and how he inspired thousands of people is told in full in the chapter "The Torch" in *Making Money Made Simple*.

Be different — most won't do it

Unfortunately, "most people" just aren't interested in self-development so if you take the time to improve your skills you will be in the minority. For example, a survey by Rybash, Roodin and Santrock looked at why 99.5% of the 3,500 workers in a truck assembly plant were not using a special education plan their union had won for them as part of a new work contract.

In this plan the company was prepared to pay for any job-related training — "training that can even include college degrees." Less than 20 people out of 3,500 bothered to take up the offer. Why so few? We have little additional information about the experiment, but let's imagine what might have happened using our knowledge of human behaviour. The workers were probably in the low wage bracket because they had a low skill level and saw themselves as being trapped in that position because they were unable to pay for further education. Most likely they blamed their low income on their lack of education in the first place, which was the fault of their parents who had not been able to afford to send them to college. They were sure their lives would change if they did have education and convinced their union officials to fight for it.

Once they won free training they had a dilemma. Lack of money for self-development was no longer an excuse and they came face to face with the harsh reality that training meant study, doing assignments, attending lectures and giving up such luxuries as "after work drinks" and a night in front of the TV. They now faced the real reason for being in a low-paid unskilled job—their own lack of motivation.

Until then, most of the workers had probably used "I can't afford it" as the excuse for not trying to improve their skills. Once that excuse was taken away it is almost certain they found other reasons not to try.

Stop reading for a moment and write down how much you spend now on such items as clothes, restaurants, coffee, movies, haircuts and junk food. Contrast it to what you are presently spending on improving your mind. If there is a huge imbalance, it might pay to consider that, in the long run, the money spent on self-development is what provides the money for the others.

Self-development takes time and effort but, as we said in the chapter on sowing and reaping, the rewards always far outweigh the effort. Only by working on your skills can you bring out the potential that is bursting inside you.

Key points:

- Move the focus from worrying about problems to finding solutions.

- The solution to almost every problem is to educate yourself to handle it better.

- When you feel better about yourself, you perform better.

- Improving your skills will improve your rewards in life.

- Opportunity favours the prepared.

- Think about the opportunity cost of watching television in contrast to spending the time on self-development.

- Only by working on your skills can you bring out the potential that is bursting inside you.

12

Failing — The essential ingredient

The freedom to fail is vital if you're going to succeed.
Most successful people fail time and time again, and
it is a measure of their strength that failure merely
propels them into some new attempt at success.

Michael Korda

The message in this chapter may scare you a bit, but it could also change your life. If you want to be successful you must expect to fail because failure is an essential ingredient in success.

Your reaction may be bewilderment. Right now you may be thinking the authors have lured me into reading almost half this book, have promised me success, and now tell me to expect continual failures. That is true, but the failures are ones that are going to help you to grow and develop your skills.

Let's think again about what we are trying to achieve. We are trying to make you stand apart from the herd and find the courage to gain the success that is your right. To do this you have to take actions to improve your knowledge and skills—in other words to move out of your comfort zone. This means trying a whole host of new things that you will probably find scary at first. These may include managing other people, handling difficult customers, taking up a sport, making a speech in public, undertaking a study course, or starting a business.

Noel says...

I vividly remember the time of departure when I made my first lecture tour on a cruise ship. I stood alone at dusk on the rear deck looking out as the great white ship left Circular Quay and slowly reversed until its stern was almost under Sydney Harbour Bridge. The decks were crowded and everybody but me seemed to be with somebody else.

The usual silly negative thoughts ran through my head. "What if nobody wants to come to my finance lectures?" "What if those who do come don't like the lectures?" None of these fears came true and the trip was a great success. The point I am making is that even though I was an

experienced speaker and traveller I was still plagued with worries. I am telling you about it here so you won't feel bad if you experience doubts and fears before trying a new experience. It's a natural feeling, but it almost always goes away once you start getting involved in what has to be done. Doubts are natural and so are failures — and I'll share some of those from my own experience too.

The only way to become competent in the area you choose is to learn about it and try to do it. Now, unless you are an exceptional person, you are not going to get it right first time. Even if you did get it right first time by some stroke of luck or genius, you would learn little by it — a real learning experience comes when it all goes wrong. It will be just like when you started to learn to walk, you tried many times, you fell over many times, but you never gave up. You kept on going and finally you made it. Sure, it was tough, but if you had not kept going you would be lying in that cot today thinking "I would love to be able to walk but if I try I might fall over and that might hurt. It's easier to stay here where it is safe and comfortable."

Finding the good in the bad

In all his books Napoleon Hill has stressed that every failure contains the seeds of a greater success. In her bestselling book *Pathfinders*, Gail Sheehy points out that successful people are not those who have been insulated from failure, they are people who have faced and overcome failure. She notes, "Repeated to a striking degree in the histories of the most satisfied adults was a history of a troubled period during childhood or adolescence. Although an unhappy childhood is not something to be wished on anyone, those who struggle through it evidently do develop important personality skills."

In her book *Mindset: The New Psychology of Success*, psychologist Dr Carol Dweck showed that the brain can be trained to grow and improve, like a muscle. Once our limiting beliefs are gradually replaced with the growth mindset (where we embrace challenges, learn from criticism, and persist in the face of setbacks), we find it easier to take actions that keep us striving for ever-greater success. This builds bulletproof confidence and creates unparalleled resilience.

The possibility of a good outcome arising from a failure may be harder for young people to grasp than it is for us older ones because life is a bit like a novel — it takes time for the reader to see how the plot develops. Those of us who have been around for a few years have had the time to watch events unfolding.

Noel says...

Let me give you three events in my own life to explain what I mean.

When I was 29 I worked for a law firm. One day there was an argument at work and I resigned in a state of temper. It was November and I was shocked to find that this is a time of the year when few companies hire new staff; they usually do it in January and February so they don't have to pay people over the Christmas break. After weeks of job hunting and a few weeks of temporary work in a factory doing process work, I finally made the shortlist for a job that I was very keen to get — it was for a credit manager at a building company.

A week later when the "we regret your application was unsuccessful" letter arrived, I leaned against the refrigerator and cried my eyes out for about an hour. I was devastated then but now, when I look back on my life, I can see that if I had got the job I would not be where I am now. Another job came my way a few weeks later that led to far more exciting opportunities.

At age 39 I went through a divorce and suffered all the pain and self-doubt that divorce usually entails. I had a few female friends to go out with but there was nobody who looked like being a contender for the love of my life. On 1 April I had arranged to go to a function with one of them but she rang to say she had "a better offer" and our date was off. Naturally, I wasn't happy about being stood up but used the occasion to go on my own to a National Heart Foundation luncheon where I met a young lady named Geraldine who was (and is) the love of my life. We are now happily married and have three beautiful children, Mark, James and Elizabeth. Also you'll find, as you persevere through relationships, that parting ways with someone, for whatever reason, is a great opportunity to reassess your goals. Like I said before, you might have your own example of how a great tragedy turned out to be one of the best things that's ever happened to you.

At one stage I got involved in a property development venture that turned terribly sour. By the time we had worked our way through the problems I had lost almost half of the material assets I had spent 46 years accumulating. In money terms, the price was huge but what I learned in that venture has enabled me to make more than I lost. I must confess it was a frightening experience but I used the technique of reframing to help me cope. I told myself it would have been much worse if one of my family had become critically ill or had been killed. Looking back I can honestly say I got more out of it than the price I paid for the "lesson".

Certainly it can be hard to handle unhappy experiences and projects that turn bad on us, but it is the most effective way we can learn. Just as a piece of iron is made hard by being plunged red hot into a tub of cold water, so a person is made tough by facing and overcoming setbacks and problems. You will never reach your potential if you try to dodge life's challenges by avoiding new experiences.

Think about the following true stories. Albert Einstein was not able to speak until he was four years old and was told by his teachers that he was too stupid to learn anything. Michael Jordan was cut from his high school basketball team because he wasn't good enough. Walt Disney was fired from a newspaper for "lacking imagination". Oprah Winfrey was fired from a reporting job after she was deemed "not suitable for television". But they stuck to their guns and went on to accomplish incredible things. What do they think of their failures?

- *Failure is success in progress.* Albert Einstein
- *I've failed over and over and over again in my life. And that is why I succeed.* Michael Jordan
- *You may not realise it when it happens, but a kick in the teeth may be the best thing in the world for you.* Walt Disney
- *Failure is a stepping stone to greatness.* Oprah Winfrey

Getting the most out of your mistakes

You will find that life continually sets you "exams" to find out what you have learned. If you fail an "exam" you are doomed to repeat the lesson until you know it. To get the most out of your setbacks, try the following:

(1) Analyse the situation and try to find out what went wrong. When you are doing this be strictly honest with yourself and don't fall into the habit of blaming others for the mishap. If you have been fired from your last three jobs or you are unable to have a compatible relationship with another person, it is likely the problem lies within you. Once you can face that, instead of trying to camouflage the real-

ity by blaming others, you are well on the way to finding permanent solutions.

(2) Practise the technique of reframing and tell yourself that what happened was obviously meant to be. Ask yourself if the incident has shown you a new direction. For example, if a job application is rejected think about whether you may be better suited to something else or acquiring different skills.

(3) Set out to find something good about the situation. For example, if you are booked for using your phone while driving treat the incident as a warning that your driving habits need attention and be thankful you were not involved in an accident.

(4) Treat a mistake as an opportunity to reassess your goals. Does this mean some of your goals are unrealistic or is the problem simply a minor detour on your path to success? For example, if you fail to gain admission to the tertiary institution of your choice you may have to consider alternative routes to get where you want to go.

(5) Be aware that failure is only a temporary condition and there are many roads leading to where you want to go. Never forget the following statement by United States President Calvin Coolidge:

> *Nothing in the world can take the place of persistence.*
>
> *Talent will not; nothing is more common than unsuccessful men with talent.*
>
> *Genius will not; unrewarded genius is almost a proverb.*
>
> *Education will not; the world is full of educated derelicts.*

> *Persistence and determination alone are omnipotent.*
>
> *The words "press on" have always solved the problems of the human race.*

This has been hanging in Noel's office since he discovered it in 1976 and it has often given him comfort when the going got rough.

While you must accept failure, if you are to succeed it is also true that you need to set up a series of successes to boost your self-esteem and put you on a success path. Therefore, while it is important that you try new things, it is also vital that you don't put too great a burden on yourself by setting almost impossible tasks. If you keep at it, you will soon learn the difference.

Key points:

- Failure is an essential ingredient in success because it helps you to grow and develop your skills.

- You will never reach your potential if you try to dodge life's challenges by avoiding new experiences.

- Failure is only a temporary condition and there are many roads leading to where you want to go.

13

Positive mental attitude

*Life is a self-fulfilling prophecy; you won't
necessarily get what you want in life, but in
the long run you usually get what you expect.*

Denis Waitley

People with a positive mental attitude expect the best
for themselves and other people in all situations.
In this chapter you will learn about the importance of
keeping a positive mental attitude and why it has such a
big effect on the way your future turns out.

The problem with the term "Positive Mental Attitude"
(PMA) is that many cynical people see it as sheer foolish-
ness. They get a mental picture of a couple dancing for joy
as they watch their house burning down with their family
trapped inside it. This attitude towards PMA may be reinforced if you attend certain types of sales meetings and
see people mouthing all kinds of optimistic slogans which,
deep down, they don't believe. They leave making positive
noises but never get around to doing what needs to be done
to make their lives successful.

Norman Vincent Peale, author of *The Amazing Results
of Positive Thinking*, explained it: "Positive thinkers do

not refuse to recognise the negative; they refuse to dwell on it. Positive thinking is a form of thought which habitually looks for the best results from the worst conditions. It is possible to look for something to build on; it is possible to expect the best for yourself even though things look bad. And the remarkable fact is that when you seek good, you are very likely to find it."

In simple terms, if you have a positive mental attitude you are an optimist who looks on the bright side of life and who expects most of the situations you face in life to have a favourable outcome. But! What if the initial outcome is unexpected, as it often is? Having PMA means you have faith that somehow the final outcome will still be a good one.

James says...

Earlier, we mentioned Dr Carol Dweck who has been a huge influence on me for all her work around the growth mindset and its evil twin the fixed mindset. Many years ago, I approached my business partner at the time with the idea of surveying our clients and our staff for some candid feedback on how we were performing, which would also identify areas for self-improvement. My business partner was so terrified of what our clients and staff might say about him personally that it took literally weeks of coaxing before he relented to the survey being released.

While the survey provided invaluable feedback that we could immediately action, it was a huge lesson for me that you need to spend as much time as possible with people who have a growth mindset and proactively seek feedback

> *on their performance so they can do better in the future. Those who are so worried about what might be revealed are the ones who will prevent any attempt to seek feedback from occurring in the first place and, even if it does, they will likely be resistant to implementing changes or discussing the feedback. They are also typically the ones who blame others for their shortfalls.*
>
> *Whether it's a business partnership, romantic partnership or a friendship, ensure that those around you have a growth mindset and are committed to self-improvement both together and individually, or you are destined for years of misery and frustration.*

Notice how what we are discussing here is closely tied in to the material in the last few chapters. You can now reframe an unexpected result to put a good face on it, you know that failure is a vital ingredient in your success, and you understand that every failure carries the seed of a greater success if you can find it. Once you combine that knowledge with the power of positive thinking, you can take action to produce the effect you want or to adjust your goals to go for a different outcome that will still be favourable to you.

We believe that having a positive mental attitude is a natural state because we have never seen a baby that didn't have a positive outlook on life. However, we seem to lose it as we get older because we become conditioned by the generally negative world around us. Because "most people" don't make it, they create a world where they will be comfortable. This is why all sections of the media prefer bad news to good news and feature the small number of bad things that happen. There is generally a headline on bad economic news or a disaster overseas, details of a car or plane crash, or a story about a murder.

You have probably noticed how the media tends to re-frame all news to the negative, which is why the headline will be "Unemployment hits 10%" and not "90% of people still have jobs".

American Senator Ed Foreman tells this story:

A young architect had just won a big contract. He went to a restaurant to have lunch to celebrate but as he sat down saw a newspaper on the next table. The huge headlines were "Depression predicted". He got such a shock that he cancelled his meal. When the proprietor asked the reason for the sudden change of heart he replied, "Look at the headlines — there is a depression coming. I had better save my money."

The restaurant owner was so surprised that he rang his wife immediately and said, "There's a depression coming. Cancel that new dress you have ordered." The wife prompt-ly telephoned the dress shop owner and told her that she had to cancel the order because there was a depression on the way. Naturally, this worried the dress shop owner and, after a quick discussion with her husband, she decided to cancel the building contract for the planned extensions to the dress shop. She rang the builder to pass on the bad news who immediately decided to cancel all the jobs he had planned for the next year. His first call was to the young architect who had started all this off, to tell him his services were no longer required because "a depression is coming".

Bitterly disappointed, the young man slunk back to the restaurant to drown his sorrows. This time he was in no hurry and picked up the paper that was still lying there. To his amazement he discovered it was an old paper dated 20 years ago and had been left there by a previous customer who had found it when he was cleaning out some old boxes. The "depression" had all been in the young man's mind, but its effects were still as real as if the paper had been printed today.

This story displays the power of negative thinking and should alert you to the importance of keeping a positive attitude. How do you become a positive person? The best way is to make it a habit but like all other habits it needs to be practised until it is firmly in place.

But how do you shift from negative patterns of thinking to more positive ones? We do not control all that happens to us, but we do control our mind and the story we tell ourselves about situations. If a business adventure (or relationship) fails, you might tell yourself you are a failure and useless. BUT, you could think of other explanations — for example, you chose the wrong franchise or partner, or you needed more financial business education, or you aimed too high or too low. There are multiple ways to view situations. There are also multiple ways to react. You might need to re-examine your goals and revise your plans to achieve them.

'Most people' believe their thoughts, "I'm dumb because I didn't get the job". We need to remember that because we think something doesn't mean it true—there might have been someone with more experience than you etc. People used to believe the world was flat thus limiting their adventures in life. Our life is what our thoughts make it. Our thoughts drive our actions. If we react in a manner that takes us towards our goal we have achieved 'a growth mindset' and a PMA.

James says...

Our feelings in life seem to come and go in waves. One day you'll have several waves of happiness but the next day you might get hit with a wave brimming with negativity and frustration. And these waves certainly aren't limited to days. Sometimes your good wave could last a week, a month or a year, but inevitably a few bad waves will roll through every now and then — that's life. Be ready for the bad waves, understand them, and your PMA will get you back on track in no time. Once you've made it a habit, teach that skill to the people you spend the most time with—especially if you're in a business partnership or a relationship with them—and you'll insulate yourself from negative energy that can get you off course.

Negative thinkers fear the worst and, therefore, subconsciously probably don't try as hard. It usually takes time and effort to produce a worthwhile result and there are often setbacks along the way. How could you possibly stick with a project if you believed you would fail?

In *Pathfinders* Gail Sheehy writes, "A person with a positive outlook is more likely to attract friendship and love which promise in turn the richer intimacy and emotional supports that characterise overall life satisfaction...people who allow themselves to become soured on life often set in motion a self-reinforcing cycle. Their anger or self-pity becomes so off-putting that it deprives them of the friends and help they otherwise would deserve."

Now think about those who have read what is in this book and are starting to put it into practice. They have set practical goals, they are discovering how to make them happen and they are working hard to develop their skills, which is building their self-esteem. They don't worry about following the crowd because they understand that "most people" are going in the wrong direction. They are not concerned about making mistakes because they know that failure is at worst an opportunity to learn and can therefore face the future with confidence. Would Kelly Slater have become an 11-time surfing world champion if he abandoned the sport after his first wipeout?

Watch how it all works together. Positive thinker's brains are putting out the right "vibes", they are being noticed because of the extra effort they are putting in, and life is steadily improving for them. As their lives start to get better they create a success pattern for themselves on which they can build. Their positive mental attitudes have helped them to do all this and, in turn, the results of their positive thinking encourage them to maintain a positive attitude.

As Albert Einstein once said, "Weakness of attitude becomes weakness of character."

Key points:

- If you have a positive mental attitude, you will not dwell on negativity. You will approach life's challenges expecting positive results.

- Practice being dismissive of negative media that does not impact on you or your interests.

- Make a habit of being mindful of what you are thinking and doing. Think about the lessons you can learn from any experience and how they can be beneficial to you in the long run.

- Choose to think and act in ways that progresses you towards your goals.

14

Give it a try

*You can't be the kid standing at the
top of the waterside, over thinking it.
You have to go down the chute.*

Tina Fey

The message in this chapter is that you should try to have as many learning experiences as possible. You may have heard the saying "luck is what happens when preparedness meets opportunity". Therefore, it should follow that the better and wider the preparation, the more chance there is for opportunity to pop up, with "luck" to follow.

Have you ever gone to the beach on a summer's day when the weather is slightly cool despite the season? The ocean looks wonderful and you walk across the sand and try the water with your toe. Feels icy. You go through the same old pattern of "Let's go in", "No, it's too cold", "Well, maybe". Then the sheer joy of the day overcomes you and you take the plunge. The first reaction might be a scream as the water hits your back, but in less than 30 seconds you are bobbing along happily saying, "How good is this!"

Most of life's situations are like that. You face a barrier and are initially put off by the apparent difficulty of it. However, you finally find the courage to cross it and then almost always discover it wasn't nearly as hard as you thought it was going to be. These barriers are important points in your life and you will keep striking them as long as you continue to grow. They are important because your reaction when you meet each one affects the way you face other barriers.

If you stop and refuse to take the plunge you are reinforcing behaviour that will probably happen again at the next barrier. You will find it harder and harder to make progress. On the other hand, if you do act, the next barrier will be easier to attack because you are forming habits that will help you make progress. As the great doctor and writer Maxwell Maltz wrote, "Close scrutiny will show that most... 'crisis situations' are...opportunities to either advance or stay where we are."

James' book *Think and Grow Rich: The Legacy* contains numerous examples of people who overcame extreme adversity. One memorable example is former champion skier Janine Shepherd who had qualified for the Winter Olympics Canada. Just a few months out from the Games, while on a bicycle training ride through the Blue Mountains, Shepherd was hit by a speeding truck. She was airlifted to hospital where her parents were told that she would not live. After 10 days in a coma, "Janine the Machine" woke up, but was forced to spend six months in the spinal ward with countless surgeries and the daunting reality that not only had her athletic hopes evaporated but her physical body was damaged beyond repair and unrecognizable.

Today, the woman who made a career out of defying the odds is a multiple bestselling author who travels the world as a walking paraplegic sharing her inspirational story with leading companies — including Amazon, Google, and Cisco — as well as non-profit associations and schools, to remind people that we are not our body but the defiant human spirit. In almost incomprehensible adversity, Shepherd was able to find the gift that has since changed the lives of millions around the world.

Noel says...

I now spend much of my time making speeches as well as doing spots on radio and television. Let me assure you I wasn't born with a talent for that; in fact I once had a speech impediment that made my early years a misery. My speaking career started at age 21 when my employer, the Bank, offered to pay for any staff who wished to improve their public speaking skills by joining Rostrum — a public speaking club. As far as I know, I was the only person who took up the offer. Everybody else was too scared of speaking in public. Naturally, I was as frightened as the rest of them but I was prepared to make the effort to learn this valuable skill.

Going to Rostrum was a terrifying experience at first, and I had a particular problem in that my knees used to shake violently whenever I got up to speak. It was hard going at first but as I persevered it got easier, and after a few months of embarrassment even my knees stopped knocking.

Time passed and through hard work and study I found myself working in the Bank's International Division dealing with foreign currencies. The Bank asked for a volunteer to give a monthly lecture on foreign currency at the staff training school. As usual, I was the only volunteer but I saw it as a further chance to develop my speaking skills and to "pose" as a VIP once a month by being driven to the school in a large, black, chauffeur-driven car.

Later, when I was running a building and real estate company, the Real Estate Institute offered six people (including me) the chance to go to Canberra for a two-day weekend course on public speaking run by the renowned speaker Doug Malouf. Three refused, but the rest of us saw it as a further chance for skill development. The course was even better than we had hoped and we all benefited greatly from it.

Learning is an exciting process because the moment you acquire a new skill, or a piece of knowledge, a chance comes up to put it into use.

Just three days after I returned from the course the ABC rang to ask if I would do a talk-back radio session for three Tuesday nights between 10pm and midnight. Naturally, I agreed and, using the knowledge I had gained at the Doug Malouf course, managed to convince the local Sunday paper to do a feature story promoting the program. I had pulled the double—the ABC and the paper were both promoting the segment. Thus, the program received maximum publicity and the phone lines ran hot.

While all this was going on I also made the time to sharpen up my writing skills by putting a weekly 400-word column in the local paper. This forced me to find a topical subject each week, write about it in an interesting way and to meet deadlines. All very useful skills.

A few weeks later another local station 4BC rang me to see if I would like to host a real estate and finance program between 6am and 7am on Saturdays. Once again I accepted the offer but figured that nobody would have the slightest interest in finance at that hour. I was wrong. Many people who are interested in finance are early risers and many others forget to turn their alarms off on Friday nights. In any event I developed a loyal bunch of listeners as I further honed up on my talkback radio skills. Even more important, I was being kept in touch with what the public needed to know.

Eventually I started writing a weekly finance column in Brisbane's The Courier Mail. *One fateful morning a woman rang the radio program to tell me she liked what I was saying and asked me to name some books in which she could read more about the topics I spoke about and wrote about. I promised her I would check out the book stores during the week and tell*

her and all the other listeners next Saturday morning.

What do you think I discovered? There was nothing in the book shops that covered finance in a simple way. Sure, there were books showing you how to turn $1 into a million quickly and easily (!!!) and thick academic books with tiny print and loads of meaningless graphs that looked too boring to open. However, there was nothing that covered the vital subject of finance in a way that enabled the average reader to benefit from it. I decided to write Making Money Made Simple, *the book which became an international best-seller and changed the lives of many who read it.*

This may have been a long story but sometimes, when I am about to give a speech to a huge audience, or get ready for a radio or television program, I wonder where I would be today if I had not accepted the bank's offer and volunteered to join that public speaking club many years ago.

Most people will never get out of their comfort level and try something new, yet it is only by trying new experiences that we can reach our full potential. It doesn't matter if the experience is helping behind a shop counter, changing a tyre, selling raffle tickets, trying 10 pin bowling or experimenting in the kitchen. Somewhere, someday, it will be useful to you even if it shows you what you ***don't*** want to do.

We'll bet when you were a child you weren't frightened to give it a try. If you were like all the children we know, you were into everything — eating dirt, running naked on the beach in winter and poking your fingers into the dog's mouth.

We just love the words of fashion designer Tory Burch "I'm always perpetually out of my comfort zone."

Now you're probably different. Now you know about fear and embarrassment and rejection and peer pressure and that daredevil-try-anything attitude has been replaced by a feeling of "What will happen if I try this and it hurts, or it doesn't work, or I end up feeling silly?"

If you feel like that, as most people do, it might be a good time to reflect on the words of William Shakespeare: "Our doubts are traitors, and make us lose the good we oft might win by fearing to attempt." When you face a new situation ask yourself, "What is the worst thing that can happen if this goes wrong?" Very often nothing more than a bit of temporary embarrassment.

Key points:

- Try to have as many learning experiences as possible.
- It is only by trying new experiences that we can reach our full potential.
- In hindsight, most things were a lot easier than they seemed at the start.

15

Universal laws

*The gifts that one receives for giving are
so immeasurable that it is almost an
injustice to accept them.*

Rod McKuen

This chapter will explain two fundamental laws that are understood and followed by truly successful people. They can be compared to the concept of love — difficult to define and measure but still very much in existence. You may question what follows, or it may confirm what you believe, but in any event it will pay to know about these laws. You may pay a heavy price if you break them.

The law of giving and receiving

James says...

The law of giving and receiving has been put in many forms. My father always told me, "If you do a good turn you'll get two good turns back." My primary school teacher taught us the Golden Rule: "Do unto others as you would have them do unto you." The Chinese philosopher Lao-Tzu said, "He who obtains has lit-

tle. He who scatters has much." I hear many people say now, "What goes around comes around." The meaning remains the same no matter how you say it.

As we outlined in chapter four, the best way to get is to give first. This is one of the most fundamental lessons of success, but unfortunately seems to be getting rarer in society.

Both of us, and most of our friends, believe in what we call the great "bank in the sky". You do good turns whenever you have the opportunity and think of them as placing deposits of good turns in some mythical bank. Then when the time comes, as it always does, that you need a good turn or a helping hand, you will find that somebody will be waiting to help you. Usually the good turns don't come from the same people you have helped, but they certainly come back. Sure, we know it sounds weird, but it works for our friends and for our family.

As your awareness grows and you continue your study of success, you will notice the concept cropping up continually. Psychologist Dr Wayne Dyer tells about the mechanic who came to his beach house to fix the refrigerator. The mechanic was loaded down with problems, which he talked about at great length. After an hour had passed Dr Dyer had given him a complete counselling session as well as numerous books and audio recordings free. The mechanic was amazed that anybody could be so generous and exclaimed, "Mister, how come you can give so much away without going broke?" Dyer smiled as he replied, "When you know the answer, you won't have to ask the question." You see he knew about the law of giving and receiving — the more you give away, the more you get back.

In *Law of Success* Napoleon Hill points out that the Golden Rule is based on the principle of sowing and reaping, which ensures that you will reap more than you sow, both positive and negative. If this is so obvious, why do so many people fail to practise it? Probably because there are two types of people — those who focus on scarcity and those who focus on abundance.

The ones who focus on scarcity see the world as a dangerous jungle. They work on the principle that everything is in short supply and only those who jump in quickly and knock everybody aside will survive. They spend their lives in constant fear — fear they won't have enough to live on, fear somebody else will beat them to a promotion, fear they will get sick. You can recognise them because their lives are in such conflict that they seldom achieve any sort of happiness.

Noel says...

I met a person with a severe case of scarcity thinking when I was giving a speech in Fiji. Contrary to popular perception, it's often lonely when you are a sole traveller far from home in some other country and I had been trying to find a golf partner to fill in an afternoon. A widow from Chicago decided to join me and we set off for the golf course that was nearly 30 kilometres from the hotel. She spent the entire journey to the course worrying if there would be a time to play available for us. When we got there she was worried that it might rain. During the round she worried all the time that she would lose her ball. And, as we neared the final hole, she expressed concern that we might not find a taxi to take us home.

On the way home she worried we might be late for dinner and during dinner she did not have a glass of wine in case she got too drunk to pack. She will never re-marry lest the new husband dies like the first one did, and she won't go out with men in case she gets hurt in a relationship. When I left her, she was concerned that all her clothes would not fit in her suitcase!

The opposites are people who focus on abundance. They have acquired a positive mental attitude that helps them to reframe a bad situation, they understand that failure is no more than a learning experience and they believe that somehow things will work out for the best. Because they feel this way, they are usually optimistic happy people who are always ready to share with others.

As you delve further into this subject you will find that most students of human success believe we attract into our lives what we focus on the most. Those who focus on abundance attract prosperity; those who focus on scarcity attract all the bad things. Do you notice how this goes round and round? Because the prosperity thinkers have an optimistic view of the world, they automatically practise the law of giving and so are assured of receiving.

One of the most famous essays in success literature is *Compensation* by the American poet Ralph Waldo Emerson. Emerson writes, "Men suffer all their life long under the foolish superstition that they can be cheated. But it is as impossible for a man to be cheated by anyone but himself, as for a thing to be and not to be at the same time."

What Emerson meant was that we can only cheat ourselves. By being too lazy or too indifferent to sow, we forfeit the great harvest we could have reaped.

The law of opposites

We call this one the law of opposites. That simply means you often have to do the opposite of what seems logical to get the result you want. Here are some examples:

- The more a farmer takes from the land, the less it returns in the long term. The way to get the most out is to put the most into it by adding resources such as water, fertiliser and mulch.

- The way to be lovable is to be loving. A person who is frantically trying to make somebody else love them is a sorry sight. It's like the child belting the kitten to make it purr.

- The harder we try to think, the less chance we have of coming up with the right answer. It will come when our minds are relaxed. You must have gone through the experience of having something you were trying to remember on the tip of your tongue and trying harder and harder to remember it without success.

Kahlil Gibran wrote, "I have learned silence from the talkative, toleration from the intolerant, and kindness from the unkind." Emerson said, "The only reward of virtue is virtue; the only way to have a friend is to be one."

At a personal development course Noel learned the best way to handle feeling unhappy was to find somebody to help, and the best way to boost self-esteem was to try to make somebody else feel good about themselves. That is probably why the happiest people we know are those who spend time helping others — they have shifted their focus off themselves and gained a feeling of usefulness.

In the section about successful negotiation in *Making Money Made Simple* Noel points out the secret of finding the best outcome is to look for a "win/win" situation where both parties get what they want. Let's look at a practical example of this in the light of what we now know about the law of opposites.

You want to borrow the family car to visit your friends, but Dad wants it to take to golf. If you both focus only on what you want, the outcome is doomed to failure. A bitter argument is almost certain to occur with Dad driving off to golf in a most unhappy state, leaving you without wheels. You will probably be miserable for the rest of the day and Dad will most likely play a dreadful round of golf and come home in a worse mood than when he left. You may then regard him as a cruel thoughtless parent and he may regard you as a problem child.

Imagine what would happen if your thoughts were focused on making sure Dad got to golf safely and in a happy frame of mind, and his thoughts were focused on ensuring you had a great day out with your friends. After a friendly talk, during which you both worked out ways to help the other gain what they wanted, you might agree that you could drop Dad at the golf course on the way to your friends' place and one of his golfing partners could give him a lift home. Everybody is happy, the outcome is satisfactory for both and the relationship is strengthened. Obviously this has huge benefits for both of you and it all happens because you choose to focus "out" and not "in".

The two laws in this chapter are a part of all religious beliefs and have been known to the human race for centuries. They are as valid now as they have always been and you will notice them occurring everywhere as your awareness develops. Your happiness will grow as you start to work with them.

Key points:

- The law of giving and receiving—the more you give away, the more you get back.
- You will reap more than you sow, both positive and negative.
- We attract into our lives what we focus on the most.
- Focus on the seeds you sow, not the harvest you reap.
- By being too lazy or too indifferent to sow, we forfeit the great harvest we could have reaped.

16

It's up to you

If you don't like the road, you're walking,
start paving another one.
Dolly Parton

This chapter could also be called "Facing Reality". Its message is that your life is very much in your hands.

That's a harsh way to start, but you must understand it if you are going to make something of your life. Read the quote at the top of this chapter again and think about it. You are where you are now because of the choices you have made to date—the smart choices and the thoughtless choices that all of us make. We are all human and have all done many positive and negative things. However, that is in the past. Where you will be in the future depends on the choices you make from now on.

When children are learning to ride a bike they usually suffer many hours of wobbling about, falling over and getting up again. Finally something clicks, it all comes together, and they have no trouble riding a bike again. Learning to take charge of your life is like that. If you continue along the path of self-development, a moment will come when you understand that you are in charge of your life. Once it clicks you will never be the same again.

Wouldn't life be scary if you weren't in control — if life was a lottery, and you had no influence over the outcome? It would be like speeding along a busy road in a car with no brakes. Fortunately, it's not like that. You do have brakes, but the road of life has hundreds of intersections and each time you come to one you have to pick which turn to make. If you keep choosing the wrong turn you end up on bad roads. Once you find yourself in the area where all the bad roads are, the situation worsens. Finally, the only choice you have is between a bad road and a worse road.

To illustrate that point, let's think about somebody we'll call Tommy who went to an overcrowded school. He could choose between paying attention in class and doing his homework, or ignoring both the teacher and the homework. He chose the lazy way and his work got behind that of his class mates. When his problems were discovered he had a choice of going to extra classes to catch up, but he chose to watch TV instead. He finally dropped out of school.

He then had the option of taking a training program, but chose to stay home. He could not get a job, got in with a bad crowd and was enticed to "borrow" a car for a joyride. He ended up in Court. He was let out on probation, but chose to break it. Eventually he was sent to jail where the only choices left to him were serving out his time or trying to escape.

Mary got her first job at 19 and had a choice of saving some money and spending what was left, or spending all of her pay and buying clothes on credit cards. Because she had chosen to borrow on her credit card to buy clothes she then faced the choice of buying no more until the debt was paid off, or increasing her borrowings. She chose to increase the debt, after all the repayments on $2,000 are only $25 a week, and continued spending as if there were no tomorrow. She was $4,000 in debt after 18 months. Her friends had been saving up to go on an overseas holiday and asked Mary to go with them. Because she had no savings, she chose to borrow another $5,000 on a personal loan.

When she returned from overseas, she got a nasty shock when she discovered how much debt she had accumulated. Her friends urged her to seek financial counselling but she chose not to. Finally, the strain became so much that she was unable to focus on her work and she lost her job.

Do you notice that both Tommy and Mary had plenty of chances to take the best road? However, each time they decided on a course of action it led to a worse road with less attractive choices. As they made more and more wrong choices, the roads got worse and so did the options available to them.

Mary and Tommy are invented characters to illustrate a point but they are typical of many young people who get into trouble slowly. The sad part is that most of those who do keep making unfortunate choices refuse to take any personal responsibility at all. They blame the "system", "other people" or might shrug it off with "that's just my luck". As you can see, luck had very little to do with it.

Notice we said "very little" to do with it because luck did play a part. Neither Mary nor Tommy had anybody to teach them they were responsible for their lives or to explain the dangers of getting into debt or being influenced by bad company.

The difference between winners and losers is that the losers believe that anything good that happens to them is a lucky break and blame everything bad that happens on somebody or something else. As a result, they never take responsibility for what happens in their lives and forever deny themselves the chance to learn.

In contrast, the winners take full credit for their successes and treat their failures as a learning experience.

The above is probably obvious when you think about it. If so, why do so many people fail to take control of their lives?

People fail to take control of their lives because:

- They don't believe they have the ability.
- They don't want to put in the effort.
- They have been conditioned to believe they are victims.
- They don't know how to get started.

We'll now think about each of these in turn and discuss ways to overcome them in the light of what we have read so far.

No faith in your ability

This is caused by a faulty self-concept that is probably the result of a previous failure pattern created by past failures in your life, or because you have always been too frightened to try anything. It can also be caused by comparing yourself to others in an unfavourable light. You may have noticed that people tend to compare their worst feature to a world figure's best feature. For example, they compare their looks to a Hollywood movie star's looks and their sporting skills to that of an international champion.

A good way to start is to stop comparing yourself with others. Then concentrate on becoming an authority on something.

The range of subjects is limitless, as the sole aim of the exercise is for you to prove to yourself you have the ability to do it. It could be running, travel writing, weightlifting, video editing, digital marketing, public speaking, or, if you are a junior in an office, knowing how to save postage. That last one might not sound too exciting, but the postage rates are confusing and nothing will get you noticed quicker than coming up with ways to save your boss money.

Once you become an "expert" in your chosen subject, and also practise the techniques described in the chapter on self-concept, you will find that your faith in yourself will grow as you start to enjoy a small measure of self-worth.

Not wanting to put in the effort

Often it has been said that winners are those who do what losers are unwilling to do. The cold reality is that making the effort is one of the factors that sets the winners apart. By now you should be aware that everything has a price but finally the rewards that come from that price far outweigh it. Do you remember Emerson's Law of Compensation from the last chapter?

From our observations, it is lack of motivation, not laziness, that inflicts so many. Why do some people who have to drag themselves to work for five days of the week leap out of bed at 4am to go fishing on Sunday morning? Where does the energy come from to party all night?

The way to overcome the lack of enthusiasm for work is to find a job you enjoy because when you have done that you have turned your work into a hobby.

Here's something to think about:

- Confucius, a famous Chinese philosopher born in 551BC, said, "If you enjoy what you do, you'll never work another day in your life." The best way to find a job you enjoy is to keep learning and finding new experiences to try until you find your niche. We've both found that we had triple the energy when we started our own businesses for, at last, the responsibilities and the rewards were for us alone. And don't be too disheartened by all the pressure that our education systems can put on us. Although you should study hard to create as many options for yourself as possible, it's not the end of the world if you don't do as well as you'd hoped on an assignment or an exam. But think about developing the habit of commitment so you can apply it to other areas of your life.

- Thomas Edison used to work 18 hours a day but once remarked, "I never did a day's work in my life. It was all fun."

- Dale Carnegie, author of one of the most acclaimed books of all time, *How to Win Friends and Influence People*, said, "Nobody is to be pitied as much as the person who gets nothing out of his job but his pay."

- Steve Jobs, the tech visionary, believed, "The only way to do great work is to love what you do."
- Simon Sinek, bestselling author and motivational speaker, said, "Working hard for something we don't care about is called stress. Working hard for something we love is called passion."

James says...

These days there is so much pressure on young people to choose a career path in their early teens and stick to it. As you've just read, if you don't enjoy what you're doing then you're very unlikely to "give it your all" or stick with it over the long term. When you're young, focus more on developing the habits, rather than a specific career, and eventually you'll find yourself attracted to something you enjoy instead of something you were forced to choose.

All progress exists outside of your comfort zone, so keep forcing yourself into challenging situations that will better your skills, such as attending seminars, networking or taking courses to communicate better. You never know what opportunities are waiting for you, but they're certainly not waiting for you in a hidden room in your house. Get out there, get a bit uncomfortable, show the world what you've got, and see how it responds.

Bad conditioning

If you have come from a family background where it is the normal practice to blame everybody else for what goes wrong, you will have to do some serious thinking. It is unlikely you will change the views of the older members of the family so you will have to compensate for their negative input with positive material from other sources.

Find some positive people to mix with and, if possible, start (or join) a mastermind group. The material listed at the back of this book will help and, as you read and understand more, you will be able to recognise any negative input from those close to you for what it is.

Not knowing how to get started

Maybe you don't know how to start. Maybe you have so many other things on your plate that you can't make the time to start. Or maybe you're just the victim of good old procrastination. Whatever it is, you should understand that starting any project is often difficult. The hardest part of writing a book is preparing the chapter outlines. Rick Everingham, the artist, believes that nothing is more difficult than staring at a blank canvas. The great Russian author Fyodor Dostoevsky said, "Taking a new step, uttering a new word, is what people fear most." The Scottish writer Samuel Smiles believed, "The reason why so little is done is generally because so little is attempted."

You start by setting practical and simple goals. Then you use the "Salami Technique" (which we mentioned in chapter nine) to make some steady progress. Once you make that first step, the rest will fall into place.

It can be difficult to move out of your comfort zone and start to accept full responsibility for your actions. However, only by doing this can you take charge of your life and direct it where you want to go. Your future is safer in your hands than in the hands of somebody else, and infinitely more fulfilling.

Making your money work

The previous chapters have focused on ways that you can realise your potential and make yourself more valuable in the marketplace. This in turn will improve your income; after all, it's the income stream that you receive during your working life that is the foundation for the wealth you will accumulate. However, all the income in the world is of no long-term benefit to you unless you put some of it away. How does a person earning $10,000 a week go broke? Simple. Spend $11,000 a week.

A detailed blueprint for turning your income into assets is given in Noel's book *Making Money Made Simple* and this should be the next book you read after you finish this one. Therefore, in the chapters that follow we will give you a brief overview to prepare you for more detailed information when you get to *Making Money Made Simple*.

Noel learnt two great lessons about money in his working life but unfortunately he was nearly 40 when he stumbled across them. You have the chance to start much earlier. These lessons are the two fundamental principles of wealth building and if you follow them it's hard to go wrong. The first is "how little things add up", the second is what we call "the Guaranteed Secret of Wealth". We'll discuss that next.

Key points:

- Your life is in **your** hands.
- Where you will be in the future depends on the choices you make from now on.
- Take responsibility and ownership for everything that happens in your life.
- There's not much to gain from comparing yourself with others.
- Making the effort is one of the factors that sets the winners apart.
- Keep learning and finding new experiences to try until you find your niche.
- Get out of your comfort zone.

17

The reality of money

If only God would give me some clear sign! Like making a large deposit in my name in a Swiss bank.
Woody Allen

In this chapter we will explain what money is and what it can — and can't — do for you.

Opportunities abound for those lucky enough to be born in a first world country, and the majority of today's young people will earn millions of dollars before they stop work. Yet, most of them will spend all their lives worrying about money and retire with nothing more than a house and a few thousand dollars in the bank.

The knowledge you have gained, and are gaining, will set you apart from "most people". When you have finished this book, you should be able to work towards a goal of complete financial security if you so desire. In the next few chapters we will show you how to make money, how to spend it and how to accumulate it. Like surfing, it's important to learn to understand surfing conditions, and then practise on the beach before you hit the waves so you can get the little things right. You don't want to jump right in and wipeout on your first investment. That's why everything before this chapter is so important—we've been building the fundamentals so that you are ready to tackle the more detailed chapters.

Before money was around, people used the barter system. You shod my horse and I gave you some eggs and butter in return. That was a cumbersome process and people found that coins were simpler as they solved such obvious problems as trying to barter a bale of hay for half a horse. The wealthier ones hoarded gold, which was usually left at the goldsmith's for safe keeping. The goldsmith gave out receipts for each bar of gold and if you needed some gold to pay a debt you went to the goldsmith, handed over your receipt, withdrew the required amount of gold and delivered it to your creditor in payment.

This was also cumbersome and the citizens found it was easier to use the receipts themselves as a means of exchange. If I owed you two bars of gold, I simply signed two of my receipts over to you. This entitled you to withdraw two of my bars of gold from the goldsmith when you wished. After a time, the receipts themselves started to act as money and eventually few holders bothered to go to the goldsmith to withdraw the physical gold.

As civilisation grew and business became more complex, banks gradually took over from the goldsmiths and finally receipts issued by banks took over from the goldsmith's receipts. Then the banks started to issue their own "banknotes" (a "note" is a term for a loan document) because it was more convenient for their customers to have money in various denominations.

However, banks are not immune from disaster and occasionally a note-issuing bank would go broke and cause huge losses to those unfortunate people who held its notes issued. One by one the government of each country took over the issuing of money and the banks gave up doing it.

As you can see, the need for convenience changed the system and it is still changing today. We now live in a society where many people hardly see money at all. Their pay goes direct into their account and they withdraw it by debit card or simply spend it direct from their mobile device. You can order an Uber and then get dropped off at your destination without ever needing to touch credit cards or cash. Despite the change in the method of completing a transaction, the essential nature of money has not changed — it is a means of exchange. It enables us to exchange our goods and services for the goods and services of others.

Unfortunately, far too many people focus solely on the money side of their life. The Bible says, "For we brought nothing into this world, and it is certain we can carry nothing out...The love of money is the root of all evil." Money cannot buy happiness, health, fine weather, contentment or good relationships, and we doubt if there are many wealthy old people who would not give up all of their wealth in exchange for being young again.

However, make no mistake about it — money is important in the areas where it works. These include providing a home, a good education, top health care, the opportunity to help others and the chance to experience the excitement of travel. What we like about money is that it enables you to make more choices in your life, choices that are based on what you want to do, not what you have to do.

Now let's consider a few basics.

Money won't make you happy

Most of us have dreamed of having millions of dollars in a bank and spending life cruising around the world or going to fancy parties. If that's your goal, and you work hard and give up enough for it, you might even get there. However, in reality most of that stuff is dreamed up by Hollywood scriptwriters and, although the fancy mansions and the huge yachts do exist, there is plenty of evidence that the lifestyle does not equate to happiness. If you want proof, look up some biographies of the so-called "glamorous people".

It came as a shock to us to discover there was almost no connection between money and happiness. The happiest person we know is a 75-year-old woman who rents a small apartment and has less than $5,000 in the bank. She was well off once but a gambling husband lost it all and left her alone to bring up a large family. She has coped magnificently with such a personal tragedy and lives a happy and fulfilled life. In contrast, we know wealthy people who are often unhappy because they don't realise that enjoying what they have is more important than the amount of money they have. Above all, it is the ability to enjoy life that makes for real happiness—this is something that can be developed if you don't have it now.

However, there is a huge connection between being unhappy and having money troubles. It is no fun to watch your car being towed away because you failed to make the payments, to arrive home to find your power has been cut off, or to lose your home because of interest rate rises.

Financial pressures can also destroy relationships. A recent study from *Relationships Australia* found that over 40% of people list "money troubles" as a major pressure on their relationship.

Why accumulate money?

Money is a medium that enables you to exchange your services for that of another. However, by itself, it is useless — if you are stranded in a burning hot desert, a suitcase full of money won't quench your thirst. What counts is what it can do for you. Having money to spend may make you feel good, it may provide a feeling of freedom or security and for many people it is even a way of keeping score.

Because you use money to pay for another's services, and you receive money by providing services, it follows that the amount of money you get depends on how much service you give. After all, money is just a product of the value you create in the marketplace. It's important to understand this.

We have reiterated that it is preferable to have control over your life. Even though money won't make you happy, building up a store of investment capital will provide financial security and enable you to have more choices in what you do. Think about the following:

(1) When you have money saved up, you can pay immediately for what you want instead of borrowing and paying interest. As most people pay hundreds of thousands of dollars in interest over a lifetime, it follows that reducing the interest you pay gives you money available for more productive purposes. For example, if Sally is paying $300 a month

in car repayments, and Anne has a car that is free of debt, Anne has $300 a month more spending money available.

(2) The investment capital you build provides opportunities for you. It is possible you will have a chance to start your own business at some stage in your life, which usually requires you to have some money to put towards it. Wouldn't it be a shame if you missed an exciting money-making opportunity just because you had neglected to build up some capital for that purpose?

(3) Building up money gives you confidence in your ability to generate income and accumulate wealth. Once you have this confidence, you know you can do it and you won't be frightened to invest some of your capital in riskier projects. Fear of loss has held many people back and it is true that, as you get older, you are less able to take large risks because you do not have the time to rebuild your wealth. If you are going to lose some money, it is better to do it when you are young. Wouldn't it be a tragedy to realise when you are old that you could have achieved your dreams, but fear of loss held you back and you didn't get around to having a go?

(4) Money gives you more freedom. Once you have established a capital base, either by accumulating income-producing investments or by building up a business, you can take a break from your job to explore other areas in your life. Certainly it takes time to get to that stage but it's a wonderful feeling to be able to take a month off to trek through the mountains or even to take a morning off to attend one of your children's sports days.

Now that you understand what money can, and can't do for you, we'll move to the principles of building wealth.

Key points:

- Financial security means more choices in life.

- There is almost no connection between money and happiness. It is the ability to enjoy life that makes for real happiness.

- Generally, the amount of money you get depends on how much service you give.

- An adequate capital base allows you to avoid interest repayments.

- Money can provide security if an unexpected emergency, such as Covid-19, comes along.

18

How to be rich!!!

*However easy it may be to make money, it is the
most difficult thing in the world to keep it.*

P.T. Barnum

In this chapter we will teach you how to start building
a fortune. It is done by the combination of slowly
accumulating capital and letting the magic of compound
interest work on it for you.

You have now read over half this book and your eyes
should be starting to open. You know you can do more than
you are presently doing to build on your potential, and that
success, whatever it means in your case, is not a matter of
chance — it requires discipline and work. Now it's time to
let you in on the secrets of building wealth.

If you've skipped over the earlier chapters and opened
straight to this page because you like the title, you've missed
out on valuable lessons and we strongly encourage you to
read from the beginning to maximise your wealth-building
potential. It will be much easier for you to grow (and keep)
your wealth if you apply the principles we've discussed
so far.

Like the other principles in this book, the secrets of
wealth accumulation are not difficult nor are they hard to

understand — it's purely a matter of getting into the habit of applying them.

Step One — Manage your money

The first key to becoming wealthy is to learn to manage your money effectively. Many people earn big money but are often broke because the money just slips through their fingers.

There is a simple and effective tool (called a "budget") for managing your money. We'll tell you about it in the next chapter. If you don't have a budget you will have no idea where your money went. Worse still, you may end up wasting most of it.

Step Two — Understand how small things accumulate

People seldom succeed or fail in one great earth shattering event. Rather, it is the succession of small things done, or not done, that makes the difference. For example, Matt saves 10% of each pay and Stephen spends a little more than he gets each pay by booking up goods on credit cards. That mightn't sound like much, but after two years Matt has $5,000 in the bank and Stephen is $5,000 in debt. They are now $10,000 apart and they are both just 21! Who would you rather be?

Sophie spends just one hour per day studying material that will improve her skills and increase her effectiveness at work, but Claire spends the same hour watching TV. It's only an hour a day, but after three years Sophie has given over 1,000 hours to study and has become a leader in her field. Claire is left wondering why Sophie is now so successful and earning double what she earns.

In 1980 Noel showed home buyers how they could save thousands of dollars in home interest by making their payments weekly or fortnightly. For example, if a couple borrows $500,000 at 7%* the repayments over 30 years are $3,300 a month—a total of nearly $1.2 million. The principal repaid is $500,000 and total interest is $700,000. Just by changing the repayments to $1,665 a fortnight, the term drops by six years and the total repayments fall by $175,000? Back in 1980 the banks all laughed at the idea but now most of them are advertising it. Better still, most homebuyers are doing it and speeding up their wealth creation process as well.

It seems like witchcraft but it's really simple if you think about it. There are 12 calendar months in a year but 26 fortnights—by making the payments fortnightly you pay back an extra $3,366 a year without realising it. Because of the magic of compound interest, discussed soon, this extra $3,366 a year makes a massive difference.

Notice one important factor. Most of the borrowers who are using this new system to save tens of thousands of dollars never had a cent to spare when they were paying monthly. They probably still haven't got a cent to spare. Nevertheless, by changing the payment frequency, they end up paying back an extra $x a year.

---

* Interest rates chosen for the purposes of the example may not reflect rates currently applicable.

Step Three — Know about the bottom line

The "bottom line" is an accounting term that refers to a company's profit. In simple terms, a profit and loss account looks like this:

Gross business income	$500 000
Cost of running the business	$450 000
Net profit	$50 000

Note: "Gross business income" is the total income before taking taxes or deductions into account.

As you can clearly see, the term "bottom line" refers to the net profit because that's where it is placed when the financial statements are drawn up.

Now think about your own little profit and loss account.

Income after tax	$60 000
Costs of your lifestyle	$58 000
Amount left over for wealth creation	$2 000

The term "costs of your lifestyle" includes food, clothes, rent, loan repayments, phone, gym, entertainment, holidays and transport — all the items on which most people spend their money. Notice that, while they are expenses you often can't avoid, they are all consumed and have no lasting value. Therefore they are not available for creating wealth. You build wealth with the money you have over.

Imagine what would happen if you could increase your net income by 10% without increasing the costs of your lifestyle.

Then your personal profit and loss account would read:

Income after tax	$66 000
Costs of your lifestyle	<u>$58 000</u>
Amount left over for wealth creation	$8 000

You have just gained a fourfold increase on the amount you have left for wealth creation by increasing your net income by 10%. Isn't that a perfect example of the law of sowing and reaping? You always reap much more than you sow.

Perhaps that sounded obvious but now re-read the section above slowly and stop and think about it. It will change your life forever if you truly understand it. We have just taught you one of the most powerful secrets of wealth in the world—increasing your income **without** increasing your costs.

What would "most people" do? Every time they increase their income, they also increase their living costs. As the British humorist Parkinson put it, "Expenditure rises to meet income." Consequently, "most people" regard an increase in pay of $4,000 as an excuse to go on a spending spree. It would never occur to them that they had just missed the opportunity to treble their investment capital. As a result, they go through life broke and will continue to blame "the system".

Step Four — Minimise borrowing for depreciating items

A major difference between financial winners and financial losers is that the winners borrow for items such as houses that gain in value, and the losers borrow for items such as furniture that drop in value. Resist the temptation to start buying goods on credit cards or through Buy Now Pay Later schemes, such as Afterpay, and avoid personal loans—if possible, delay buying a car if you have to borrow for it. Use the family car, a ride-sharing company (such as Uber or Lyft), or public transport for as long as possible. .

Step Five — Appreciate the importance of increasing your income stream

Think of financial independence as a destination and the assets you accumulate along the way as the vehicle to get you there. The income you earn is the fuel that drives the vehicle — the more you can earn, the faster the trip will be — provided you use the income for wealth creation and not for consumer spending.

Unfortunately "most people" seem to believe the more you make, the more tax you pay, and therefore it is not worthwhile making the effort. Deep down they are probably too lazy to stretch themselves to provide the extra service to make the extra money. It's a stupid way to think, whatever their reasoning. There are many legal strategies that can minimise tax, particularly if you have your own business or have investments.

Step Six — Use your income to acquire assets

You now know the importance of putting money aside for wealth creation. It can be done in two ways:

(1) By saving the money you have left over after paying your tax and your living expenses, or

(2) By using tax-effective borrowing.

The formula

(1) To build wealth, you first have to produce income. You do this by improving your skills.

(2) Don't spend all you earn. Make sure you keep some to invest. It's your money, so why give it to someone else?

(3) As your investment capital grows, it too will produce income. Now you have two sources of income — from your assets and from your work.

(4) As your assets grow, use them, plus the money they are making for you, to buy more income-producing assets.

Naturally it takes time, particularly in the early stages, but you will discover in the next chapters that the process gets faster and faster as time goes by. But it will never start unless you earn money and keep some of it to invest.

 Key points:

- The secrets of wealth accumulation are not difficult. It's purely a matter of getting into the habit of applying them.

- Learn to manage your money effectively.

- It is the succession of small things done, or not done, that makes the difference.

- Learn how to increase your income without increasing your costs.

- Borrow for items that appreciate in value, not the other way around.

- Don't spend all you earn. It's your money, why give it to someone else?

- Cultivate multiple sources of income to boost your wealth.

19

Budgeting

Balancing your money is the key to having enough.
Elizabeth Warren

This chapter will teach you the importance of having a system to keep your finances on track and to prevent you frittering your money away.

The early chapters in this book concentrated on helping you improve the way you manage yourself to ensure you develop your personal potential. The next few chapters will show you how to manage your money so you get the best out it. There is little doubt you will earn a higher than average income if you follow the principles in this book but there is not much to be gained by having a high income if you waste every cent of it. The solution is to form the habit of managing your money properly.

First, you have to understand what is really meant by a budget. It's explained in full in *Making Money Made Simple* and you can study it in detail when you read that book. In this chapter we'll just give you the basics.

The first pay

Let's start with the fundamentals and imagine you have found your first job, are still living at home or in shared accommodation, and have just received your first pay. Congratulate yourself, you have taken a vital step to independence by earning some money of your own. You have just turned on a tap from which millions of dollars are going to gush in your lifetime — it's like finding an oil well in your backyard that will support you for life. You are now on the road to wealth, provided you develop a few simple habits.

This may be a fitting time to reflect once more that "most people" never get to learn about these habits, much less practise them. They will also earn millions of dollars in their working life, but will be constantly broke and will finish up with their hands stretched out for the welfare cheque. The techniques in this book will give you the opportunity to live differently if you start to practise them.

Because you are young, your first pay probably won't be big and the natural reaction is to say to yourself, "I'll spend all of this but when I start to earn big money I'll put a plan in place to manage my money properly and make it grow." If you start thinking like that you will join "most people" who continually say, "If I win the Lotto I'll start to take care of my money." It's an irony because, if they had always taken care of their money, they wouldn't be worried about winning the Lotto today. They're the same people who say "If I had a good body I'd look after it."

Do you see, now, how it all works together? Life's losers say they will go the extra mile at work **after** they get the promotion, and manage their money properly **after** they become wealthy. Unfortunately, for them, life doesn't work like that.

It's not the money that counts, it's the habit. Therefore, you should look upon that first money you earn as giving you an opportunity to start developing good habits that will give you an edge on everybody else.

The major goal is to get into the habit of living within your means, something "most people" never do. When people spend even just a little more than they earn, they have to borrow small amounts to get by. This way of going into debt is like contracting a slow creeping disease. It is so important that we have devoted two chapters to it in this book.

Well, there's the ankle-deep loan that drags on forever, the knee-deep loan that seems endless or the neck-deep loan that's really scary for a few years less.

Your other goal should be to save a portion of each pay. How much? If you are living at home, probably 20% of your net pay is reasonable. It is easier to save a larger part of your income while you are living at home and can get cheap board and perhaps the use of the family car.

Now we know that saving $120 a week out of a wage of $600 will seem like chicken feed and probably after a few weeks you'll look at your bank balance of a few hundred dollars and wonder if such small amounts of savings are worth worrying about.

Let's repeat the secret — it's not the money, it's the habit. Most of your peers will save nothing, or worse still, will already be starting to acquire the habit of depending on credit cards. By saving 20% of your take home pay and living within your means, you will put a habit in place that will virtually guarantee you will be one of the few people who become wealthy.

However, you have to beware of the power of human nature — we tend to spend whatever we get. Ask around and you will find that almost all your friends, and their parents and their friends, have trouble living on their incomes even though they all have different incomes.

The trick is to have the 20% you wish to save deducted from your salary and paid straight to a special account with your bank, building society or credit union. If you do that, and put money away in another account for essential expenses, you can spend the rest on clothes, holidays, entertainment, restaurants and having fun with a clear conscience.

This is also a good time to practise your newly acquired knowledge of setting goals. Why not plan to have a special holiday in 12 months time? Work out the cost of it, open a special holiday account, and put in part of the cost each week. Start that habit now and you are assured of good holidays for the rest of your life.

Now you understand the theory of budgeting, let's move to the practical part and prepare one. It is simply a matter of preparing a schedule that lists your income followed by the items on which you wish to spend your money. We have shown a sample budget and you will notice the items are listed in order of priority, with "savings" at the top of the list and all the "fun" things at the bottom.

The "fun" items, such as entertainment and travel, are at the bottom because at a pinch you can do without them. They are not as important to your future as savings, fares and food. Unfortunately "most people" spend on the fun things first and find there is never anything left over for savings. Then they promise to start "next week" which of course never comes.

Budget — per week

Income after tax	$600
ESSENTIAL ITEMS	
Savings a/c	$120
Holiday a/c	$50
Transport	$40
Grooming	$10
Cost of Accommodation	$40
Self-Education Expenses	$20
Total essential items	$ 280
BALANCE REMAINING FOR	
Clothes	
Movies	
Restaurants	
Entertainment	
Etc., etc., etc.	$ 320

After just 12 months there will be over $6,240 in the invest-
ment savings account and over $2,600 in the holiday ac-
count when interest is credited. Can you imagine how good
it will feel to know you have saved nearly $9,000 in your
first year of working?

If you understand the power of budgeting, you will quickly establish yourself as a person who can manage money
and who can set and achieve goals. The result will be more
than a future free of financial problems — it will almost
surely mean a great sense of wellbeing and self-esteem.

Key points:

- It's not the money that counts; it's the
  habit.
- Beware of the power of human nature
  — we tend to spend whatever we get.
- Prioritise your expenses to identify areas where you can save money.
- Get into the habit of going the extra
  mile.

20

Understanding interest

Time is your friend, impulse is your enemy. Take advantage of compound interest and don't be captivated by the siren song of the market.
Warren Buffet

"Interest" will make you or break you. Therefore, if you are going to get ahead in this world you will need to understand the concept of interest and use it to build your wealth. However, interest is like fire — a good servant but a bad master. In this chapter you will learn how to make it work to your advantage and how to keep away from the dangers.

A good way to define interest is "the price paid by somebody who borrows money to somebody who lends it".

There are three areas in which people invest the bulk of their money. In each case the investment gives the person with the money a benefit. The three areas are:

(1) Money lent out to institutions such as banks, finance companies, building societies and credit unions who, in turn, lend it to people who wish

to borrow money. The borrowers pay interest in return for the use of the money.

(2) Real estate, which gives you free shelter if it is your own home, or provides you with income by way of rent if you are a landlord.

(3) Shares in companies. The shares usually provide the investor with a share of the profits in the company by paying profits out as "dividends".

As you can see, if you have money to invest it can be made to give you benefits. These benefits may be more income (through interest, rent and dividends), or in the form of free accommodation (if you buy a house). However, if you are receiving money, there must be somebody else paying it out. Obviously it makes sense to be getting it **in** rather than paying it **out**. To help you understand this, we'll follow a money trail to show you how it all comes together.

How to make interest work for you

Ted and Alice are retired and have over $600,000 in cash. They "deposit" the money in an account at the XYZ Bank and receive interest at the rate of 4%* per annum. This means that every year the bank pays Ted and Alice $24,000 for the privilege of being able to use their money.

Lachlan and Katie are a young couple who have always wanted a home of their own. They have been saving as fast as they can for this home and have accumulated $150,000 in the XYZ Bank. It is paying them 4%* interest as well. But there is a problem. They have discovered the amount they can save, even with the benefit of the interest the bank is paying them, is not increasing as quickly as the growth in

---

* Interest rates chosen for the purposes of the example may not reflect rates currently applicable.

house prices. The only way they can solve the problem is to use somebody else's money to help them buy the house.

The house they want is now selling for $750,000. After some serious discussion, they decide to take the plunge and borrow $600,000 from the bank to use to buy the house. They pay the bank 6%* for the use of the money, although you could say they are using Ted and Alice's money with the bank acting as the go-between.

Everybody is doing well out of the deal. The retired couple are gaining interest for allowing somebody else to use their money, and the young couple now have a house even if it does have a big mortgage. The bank is doing well too – it is paying Ted and Alice $24,000 for the use of the money and collecting $36,000 from Lachlan and Katie. The profit of $12,000 is used to pay the costs of running the bank, such as staff wages and rent, and the balance is paid to the bank's shareholders as dividends.

You can see now the concept of interest has enabled Ted and Alice to earn money to live on in retirement and it has also helped Lachlan and Katie to buy a house. It's a win/win situation.

Notice another important point. The only reason Lachlan and Katie borrowed the money was to enable them to buy the house today instead of waiting for a date in the future when the house might cost more. The interest they pay is the price of doing this, but how large a price is now up to them. It is not like buying a Big Mac where you know the price when you walk into McDonald's. They will continue to pay interest to the bank until the entire loan is paid back.

A smart way to invest money

If Lachlan and Katie choose to pay it back over a long term, say 30 years, they will have to repay $2,147 a month.

Because of the long term of the loan, the repayments in the early years are mainly interest. In fact, in the first month the bank keeps $1,667 of that $2,147 payment for interest, which leaves only $480 a month for reducing the loan balance. Even after five years they still owe $367,000.

If they had kept repaying $2,147 a month for 30 long years, Lachlan and Katie would have paid back $373,000 interest as well as the original sum of $400,000 – a total of $773,000. The price of borrowing the money to enable them to buy that house today has been over three quarters of a million dollars. That's huge!!

There is more bad news. As you learn more about investment, you will discover that interest paid on a loan for your own home is not allowed as a tax deduction in many countries. Therefore, you make your housing repayments from that part of your income that is left after tax has come out. These remaining dollars are called "after tax dollars". Lachlan and Katie would have to earn over $612,000 just to produce the after tax dollars to pay that interest bill of $373,000.

Luckily Lachlan and Katie are educated borrowers. They had read Noel's books, were aware of the way interest worked, and had decided to take control of the situation by using all their efforts to pay off the loan quickly. They both worked and repayments of $4,000 a month were within their capacity.

Their loan is now down to a level where it can be handled easily on one income, but if they maintained repayments of $4,000 a month the loan would be repaid in 10 years with just $119,000 of interest.

The extra payments saved them $254,000 of after tax dollars in interest. That's the equivalent of their earning an extra $417,000 of pre tax dollars!! Can you think of an easier way to earn $417,000?

A silly way to spend interest

Lachlan and Katie saved thousands of dollars in interest because they were smart enough to invest in an asset that will grow in value and because they knew how much they could save by paying their loan back quickly.

Tom and Jess took a different approach. They decided to buy a car. They had never been savers so took out a loan of $40,000 to cover the entire purchase price. They decided to go for the longest term to keep the repayments down to a level that would allow them plenty of money left over to spend on clothes, nights out and travel. They let the car dealer arrange the finance and found themselves borrowing $40,000 over five years at 12%. The monthly repayment came to $890 and they paid back a total of $53,400 over the five years. The interest bill alone amounted to $13,400 much of which could have been avoided if they had saved a large deposit and paid the loan back over a shorter term.

How delay affects interest

If you are a borrower, the three factors that influence the total interest you pay are:

- ✔ The amount borrowed
- ✔ The interest rate, and
- ✔ The amount you repay each year.

You will learn in the next chapter (on compound interest) about the importance of starting early, but you should also understand that a few years delay in buying an item that is growing in value could cost you dearly.

For example, when she was 25, Amanda bought an apartment for $350,000 with a $50,000 deposit. She borrowed $300,000 and paid it back over 15 years at $2,372 a month. By her 40th birthday the unit was paid off. Her total repayments (principal and interest) were $427,000.

Peter waited till he was 30 and then paid $400,000 for a similar property because prices had risen. He also put down $50,000 deposit, but had to repay $2,310 a month because he borrowed $350,000. The term of the loan was 20 years and his total repayments were over $554,000.

Let's now assume that Amanda, having paid off her unit, now invests $2,310 a month – the same amount that Peter is paying on his mortgage. Contrast where the pair of them will be at age 50. Amanda not only has a mortgage-free home but may also have accumulated over $422,000 from her investments. Peter, however, will be making his final home payment.

What interest does

Interest is the price you pay to get some money to use today if you are short of money. You should ask yourself: "Is it worth paying a price to have spending power available now?" Only you can answer that question but you will find most people borrow money for one of four reasons:

(1) They want to buy an expensive asset (such as a house) and believe it is better to buy now before prices go up.

(2) They need the use of a depreciating asset (such as a washing machine, furniture or a car) now and don't have the money available.

(3) They want to indulge themselves with a holiday or big-screen TV but don't have any available savings.

(4) They have pressing expenses (such as the electricity bill) to pay but have no money put aside because of never managing their money properly. They will suffer unpleasant consequences if the money is not found somehow.

As these topics are covered in detail in *Making Money Made Simple* we will not explore them in detail here. Notice you could argue a case that it is acceptable to borrow for the first two reasons. However, if anybody has to borrow for the last two reasons it is obvious they are not practising budgeting or that they suffer from a lack of control.

How interest can help you

Once you have money saved up, you can invest it and receive interest on it. This means you have increased your income because you now have interest coming in, as well as the other income from your work — you've cultivated multiple sources of income. In the next chapter you will see how the miracle of compound interest can make your savings grow at a faster and faster rate.

If you have to spend money on interest, one of the best ways to become wealthy is to buy real estate. Probably the real estate you know best is the house or apartment in which you live. If your parents have been following Noel's advice about paying off the loan on the property quickly, they may now own the property without any mortgage.

Stop and think about the benefits of that for a second.

No loan repayments to make, no rent to pay and no fear of being kicked out in the street if the landlord decides to sell the property. That's what we call a feeling of security.

However, even if they own the house now with no mortgage, it is highly likely they borrowed money when they bought it originally. They may have been paying rent of $400 a week and discovered this was nearly as much as the repayments on a home. They decided to buy a place of their own, instead of being at the mercy of landlords for the rest of their life. They had to make an important decision — do they keep on paying rent and try to save the full price of a house, or do they use the money they have as part payment for the house and borrow money for the balance? Luckily they took the plunge and bought the house.

You should now appreciate that interest is the price you pay to spend money you don't have. Once you start to borrow, you are promising to pay a part of your future income to another person who is the source of the money that has been lent to you. Whether the price is justified is a matter only you can decide.

Key points:

- Interest is the price you pay to spend money you don't have.

- If you are a borrower, the three factors that influence the total interest you pay are the amount borrowed, the interest rate and the amount you repay each year.

21

Compound interest

Do not despise the bottom rungs in the ascent to greatness.
Publilius Syrus

Get ready—in this chapter you will have a mathematics lesson. Don't let the topic scare you off because it may well be the most profitable maths lesson you have ever had.

Financial textbooks often refer to the "magic" of compound interest because what happens when you use it appears to be truly miraculous. You read in a previous chapter that interest is a fee that is paid to you for the hire of your money, and paid by you when you want to hire somebody else's money. The interest is usually paid by the borrower to the lender on a regular basis. Generally this is monthly, but it may be quarterly or even yearly.

However, there is another way for a lender to receive interest—it may be added to the principal (the amount already owing) and left to grow. This is called compounding the interest because the principal is then bigger as a result of the compounded interest. Do you notice how, when this happens, the borrower is paying interest on interest?

This interest on the interest may also be compounded and, when the next lot of interest is due, it is also added to the principal and the compounded interest. Now the poor old borrower is paying interest on interest on interest.

This is how it works:

Loan $10,000

Interest rate 10%

Interest is due each year and is compounded by being added to the principal.

Year 1

Original sum borrowed	$10 000
Interest for first year	$1 000
Balance owing end of Year 1	$11 000

Year 2

Opening balance	$11 000
Interest for second year	$1 100
Balance end of Year 2	$12 100

Year 3

Opening balance	$12 100
Interest for third year	$1 210
Balance end of Year 3	$13 210

That all looks innocent, doesn't it? It may, until you analyse the figures. After just three years, the borrowers owe 32% more than they originally borrowed. Moreover, the interest bill in the third year is 21% more than the interest for the first year. It's often been called "creeping into big trouble".

You can work out the effect of compound interest by using the Rule of 72. This miraculous little trick works with any interest rate. Write down the number 72 and divide it by the interest rate. The answer is the number of years for the amount you owe to double. If we use 10% from the example on the previous page, it looks like:

$$\frac{72}{10\%} = 7.2 \text{ years}$$

Using the Rule of 72 we have now calculated that $10,000 would double in just over seven years if the interest was allowed to compound instead of being paid to the lender at regular intervals. Therefore, after 7.2 years the borrowers would owe $20,000 instead of the $10,000 they borrowed at the start.

Let's go a step further and imagine we left the money untouched for another seven years. The debt would double again. Now the hapless borrowers would owe $40,000. That's right—in just 14 years, because of compound interest, the borrowers would owe four times what they borrowed in the first place. Leave this compounding process for another seven years and the debt is $80,000.

Think about that for a minute.

The $10,000 has grown to $80,000 in just 21 years. It has increased by 800%. That's an average of 38% each year on the original sum.

Notice how compounding starts slowly, but gets faster and faster and faster. It is just like an avalanche that may start with a few stones sliding down a mountain and picks up speed and size as the stones collect rocks. These rocks in turn collect huge boulders until the avalanche is like a torrent of stone pounding down the slope.

"How does this affect me?" you may be thinking. It affects you in two ways. Once you understand the principles of compound interest, you can avoid being trapped into dangerous levels of debt by compound interest. **And** you can also use the knowledge to slowly build a fortune. This is because it can speed up the rate at which your money grows. Suppose your grandparents invested $5,000 a year for you into an index fund starting on the day you were born. If the fund returned 9% per annum, the end of year values would be:

End of Year 5	$30 000
End of Year 10	$76 000
End of Year 15	$130 000
End of Year 20	$256 000
End of Year 25	$424 000
End of Year 30	$682 000

Notice how the growth for the first five years is only $5,000, in the second five years $21,000 yet in the last five years $233,000. There is almost as much growth in those last five years as there was in the first 20 years.

This is why it is so important to start building your wealth at a young age.

The problem for "most people" who try to build wealth through compounding is that the compounding process starts slowly and they tire of it before it has had a chance to work. Then they cash in the investment and blow the money on a holiday or a car.

Another secret of wealth

Unfortunately, income tax can punch a hole in your plans because many countries have progressive tax systems; that is, the rate of tax rises as your income rises. However, when you buy an asset such as property or shares, any capital gain automatically is added to the asset value without any action on your part. As a result, the compounding process is automatic and no capital gains tax is payable until the asset is sold.

A clever way to wealth, which is used by most serious investors, is to borrow money for the asset and to pay the interest regularly instead of letting it compound. When they do this, the asset value should grow faster and faster because of the compounding effect. At the same time, the debt will remain static and the investors' equity (the difference between the asset value and the loan) will grow.

Let's use some simple figures to illustrate the point. Imagine an investor bought an investment property for $350,000 using a deposit of $50,000 in combination with an interest only loan of $300,000. The deposit is called the "investor's equity". If the interest on the loan was $21,000 a year and the net rents from the property were $21,000 a year, the investor could sit back and let the tenant pay the interest as the income was covering the outgoings. If the house doubled in value in 10 years, and the loan balance did not drop, the investor would then have a $700,000 house with a $300,000 loan. The initial equity of $50,000 has grown to $400,000 ($700,000 house value minus $300,000 loan = $400,000).

What has always fascinated us about compound interest is that it works in ways that seem totally illogical.

Think about two young people beginning separate investment programs for their retirement. The first starts putting $2,000 a year away at age 19 but stops at 26.

The second does not start until age 26 but then invests, without fail, $2,000 a year till age 65.

Who do you think will end up with the largest sum of money (assuming a 10% rate of return)?

Strange, though it may seem, the winner is the first one who contributed only $14,000 but ended up with $945,000. The loser is the one who delayed and finished with $894,000 for a total investment of $80,000.

We hope this lesson on compound interest has got you fired up and ready to go. Don't forget that it takes time to work and that you need money to use it. Our next lesson will show you how to make that money.

Key points:

- Start building your wealth as early as possible.

- The Rule of 72 (72 divided by the interest rate) calculates the number of years it takes for the amount you invest to double.

- Understanding compound interest can help you avoid being trapped into dangerous levels of debt and can also help you to build a fortune.

22

The guaranteed secret of wealth

Being rich is having money;
being wealthy is having time.
Margaret Bonnano

Our attitude to money is like our attitude to time—we always find time to do the jobs we have to do but then find there is nothing left for anything else. We might not have time for exercise in the morning but we do have time for a shower. We may not have time to go to the gym but we do have time to go out partying with friends.

Doesn't it follow that the only way to make sure we do the things we have to do is to prioritise them? Does that not lead to the logical conclusion that the only way to become wealthy is to make investing a priority? Noel called that "revelation" the Guaranteed Secret of Wealth.

While you might agree that it's important to make investment a priority, you may also feel that with all the calls on your income it's easy to overlook it (a "call" is any part of your life, good or bad, that requires short-term financial attention). This is what Noel's Guaranteed Secret of Wealth is all about—making investment a priority and doing it in such a way that it happens automatically.

Remember we told you that up to 1980 or so everybody made their home loan repayments monthly. That was until Noel stirred up the banks by going on national TV and telling people they could save a fortune in interest if they made their payments weekly or fortnightly instead. All the banks scoffed at the idea. They claimed that, because the interest was charged monthly, paying weekly or fortnightly made no difference.

The banks had missed the point. It didn't have a thing to do with when the interest was charged.

It's worth revisiting the example we gave you in the chapter 18. Think about a couple paying back $3,300 a month on a $500,000 housing loan over 30 years. They will almost certainly go through the following process — they will get paid, put aside the money for the loan repayments, spend the rest and arrive at next pay day broke.

Look at what happens when they move to fortnightly payments. They still get paid, put aside the money for the loan repayments, spend the rest and arrive at next pay day broke.

Nothing has changed. Or has it?

Now they are paying $1,665 a fortnight instead of $3,300 a month. But, there are 26 fortnights in a year and only 12 months. Annual payments have risen from $39,600 (12 x $3,300) to $43,290 (26 x $1,665) with the result that the loan term has dropped by seven years and they have saved over $175,000.

What is different? Nothing, except that by using a smart strategy, they were compelled to pay an extra $37 a week off their home loan. Did they find the extra payments a burden? Not at all! Did it make a difference to their financial wellbeing? A massive difference! $175,000 in interest saved, and the loan paid nearly seven years earlier.

That's the first principle: "You don't miss what you don't get".

Surely it follows that if you have your investment money deducted automatically you won't miss it either. All banks nowadays have internet banking facilities in place so you can easily manage your finances online. Create a special savings account and, as soon as you can, transfer the amount you would like to save for a special purchase like a car, a holiday, a share portfolio or even a house. It's an easy lesson to learn when you see what happens to savings that are left in your everyday account — they get squandered on everyday items that you won't even be able to remember at the end of the month.

Now let's think about another real-life situation. Ten people go out to dinner at a fancy restaurant and the bill comes to $1,000. One member of the party puts the entire $1,000 on her credit card and the other people give her $100 each. She goes home with a $1,000 debit on her credit card and an extra $900 in her wallet. That's fair, isn't it? What do you think will be the situation in four weeks time when the credit card statement with the $1,000 restaurant bill on it comes in? Do you really think she'll still have that $900 in her pocket? Chances are it has been frittered away on everyday items that were of no long-term use.

That's the second principle: "Money in your wallet just goes." (While obviously saving us time, the rollout of contactless payment, such as PayPass, PayWave and Apple Pay, can be categorised as a "wallet" too.)

A wonderful illustration of the Guaranteed Secret of Wealth at work is the behaviour of borrowers in the late 1980s when housing interest rates jumped. Interest rates went to record levels and, naturally, mortgage repayments went up too. This stretched the budgets of many households, but less than 1% of people lost their homes. The rest managed to cope with the burden of the extra payments, and the smart ones kept up the higher payments when rates inevitably fell again.

Do you know why most people didn't let the bank foreclose on their mortgages? Because they knew the importance of keeping the family home. It is their shelter and the focus of family life.

Saving for the future is just as important — the problem is that it is not immediate. Delay the investment program for a week, a month or even three years, and the sky won't fall in.

But, all of a sudden, age 45 comes around, and you start to think of retirement as something that may be just 120 months away. The moment you do the calculations you face the unpleasant truth that you have let time get away from you. Now it's a matter of starting a massive savings program for the next 10 years, or delaying that long-awaited retirement until age 60 or 65. All because you didn't get around to practising the Guaranteed Secret of Wealth.

Now that you understand the way the Guaranteed Secret of Wealth works, find ways to put it into practice. For example, simply arrange internet banking facilities so you can save the money you want to. As soon as it enters your everyday account, transfer it to your special untouchable account for future use.

For the readers who have an existing home loan, simply pretend that interest rates have just risen by 2% and raise your loan repayments accordingly. In a month or so, you will be used to the extra payments and you will have given yourself a safety buffer if rates rise. If they don't, you will save tens of thousands of dollars in interest.

If you don't have a home loan yet, ask your employer to deduct at least 15% of your income from your pay and have it credited to a bank account. You won't miss it and, as the weeks pass, you will be amazed at how quickly it grows.

Key points:

- Make investment a priority and do it in such a way that it happens automatically.
- You don't miss money you don't get.
- Money in your wallet gets blown on everyday items.
- Put the Guaranteed Secret of Wealth into practice.

23

How to earn more money

Everything you want in life has a price connected to it. There's a price to pay if you want to make things better, a price to pay for leaving things as they are, a price for everything.

Harry Browne

In every country there is a massive gap between the income earned by the lowest and the highest paid people. In this chapter you'll learn why this is so and what is needed to put yourself in a higher income bracket.

Money is a medium that lets one person exchange goods and services for that of another. Therefore, it should be obvious that the more goods or services you can offer, the more money you are likely to receive in exchange. However, some goods and services are worth more than others. A shop assistant provides services, yet earns less for an hour's work than a teacher who may earn less than a plumber who, in turn, receives less than a doctor. Do you find this confusing? Not one of these individuals is any better than any other, and they all fill essential roles in our community. Why the difference in remuneration?

Here is the formula. The amount of money you are paid depends on:

(1) The demand for your services.

(2) How well you do what you do.

(3) The difficulty in replacing you.

James says...

Steve Jobs, co-founder and former CEO of Apple, was one of the innovators of modern information technology. In the 1970s and 1980s, he was instrumental in the development of personal computers and the evolution of the IT industry. Now think about that in the context of the three points we discussed earlier — Jobs was in enormous demand, he was a leader in his field and would likely be very difficult to replace. Nonetheless, in 1985 the corporate structure of Apple squeezed him out and he was forced to pursue other interests.

Rather than dwell on his misfortune, Jobs saw this as a great opportunity and founded another IT company, which ended up being so valuable that it was purchased by Apple in 1996 for almost half a billion US dollars. History had proved that Jobs was irreplaceable and, in the mid-90s, he returned to Apple as CEO.

If you think about the above for a while, you may decide that being very good at what you do is the area on which to concentrate. That is the one over which you have most control. Also, if you are particularly good at what you do, the other two will fall into place naturally because your services will be in demand and you will certainly be hard to replace.

Now, you may think this pay system is a bit unfair. You might think the highest paid people should be school teachers or university lecturers because they have the responsibility of educating our next generation. You may feel doctors are most important because they can save lives and help bring babies into the world.

That might be fine in theory but in real life the system doesn't work like that. Your income is determined not by fairness but by the market. A popular author might write absolute garbage, but will be highly paid if enough people like to read what he or she turns out. Some television stars may receive a huge amount of money for making five 30-minute appearances every week. A sporting hero may earn a million dollars in one match. A rock group might receive more for a two-hour concert than most people earn for a year's work. That happens because there is a huge demand for their services and skills.

Noel says...

A friend of ours owns a jewellery shop. When you walk into that shop, a woman, Mary, stands out. She has a bright look in her eye, is always happy and smiling, knows all the regular customers by name and is wonderful to deal with. Recently, I asked the owner how long she had been there. He replied, "Over 10 years and she is priceless. If she left I could not replace her." I have no doubt Mary receives a much higher salary than most other shop assistants and that she would be swamped with offers if she ever decided to leave her present job.

Think about the other side of the coin, for it contains a valuable lesson for you. The **majority** of authors, television personalities, sports professionals and musicians are in the lowest paid ranks of the workforce because so many people want to get into those "glamour" industries. They all want to make it big, but only a tiny number reach the top. Those that do are at the absolute peak of their profession. They are the best at what they do — at least in the public eye. Throughout the world there is a range of talent quests. Many of them are extremely popular and revolve around the basic premise that only one person will win the competition and become famous. Have you ever wondered what happens to the tens of thousands who apply but don't win the competition? Apart from being forgotten very quickly by the viewers, they are usually destined to keep struggling with improving their craft to crack the big time. For many, this can be a very lonely existence.

All markets operate on the theory of supply and demand. The more people there are seeking the same kind of work, the less any one of them is likely to be paid. If you are a migrant with no specific skills and can hardly speak the local language, you may well end up doing process work in a factory where you are in danger of being replaced by a robot. Think about what would happen if you spent your entire working life with the one organisation in an administrative role and were then retrenched at the age of 50. It could be very difficult for you to find another job.

It is often easier to find jobs if you are prepared to travel to remote areas because few people want to go there. A friend of mine is now aged 65 and his services as a cost accountant are still in high demand because he will work in remote places.

Remote jobs usually pay more than the equivalent position in the city and saving is easier in those places because there is often little to spend your money on. Many clients of financial planning firms received their financial start in life by working in the country or in one of those non-glamorous overseas areas. They set a goal to spend five years there, work long hours and build up a large sum of investment capital.

Now that you understand the relationship between employment markets and supply and demand, you will appreciate the importance of improving your skills. This will help you to become a member of the elite band whose skills are in demand, instead of being just another member of a large group chasing any job you can get. The top people in their fields always have job security as well as higher than average incomes.

You've got to put in the hours

Throughout the book we have stressed the importance of self-development and going the extra mile because this will enable you to develop the skills that will put you at the top of your chosen field. In the next chapter we will show you how to "multiply" yourself and move into the really high-earning field by progressing toward having your own business. However, when you are starting off, there is just no substitute for putting in the time.

The good news is that when you find the right path for yourself, the long hours don't matter because you will be enjoying what you do. Noel started writing this chapter at 4.45 on a Saturday morning in December, just a week before Christmas. He was holidaying at the beach and was sitting with his laptop on a patio overlooking the surf. The rest of the family was sleeping peacefully but he couldn't think of anything he would rather be doing.

After getting harassed by fans asking him for advice on how they too could build their own army of fans, marketing guru Gary Vaynerchuk wrote the article "Stop Asking Me About Your Personal Brand and Start Doing Some Work". In it he wrote, "There is no substitute for honest, hard work. If you want something badly enough, come up with a plan and get to work because, like compound interest, it's a long, slow grind to the top, but the rewards are well worth it."

What if you don't like working long hours? Find a hobby that you love doing, or are passionate about, and try to build a business around that. We have stressed that there is no connection between money and happiness, and you may have to settle for lower earnings if the field you enjoy does not return a huge income. If that is the case, go for what you enjoy.

Remember what we've discussed earlier — your rewards in life will match your service; therefore, the more time you put into developing your skills and providing service, the greater your rewards will be. Even if these rewards come in the form of personal satisfaction instead of money, you will have a fulfilled life.

How to score a promotion

We will now let you inside an employer's mind and show you how to carve a fast track up the ladder of success. Let's pretend you are the owner of a small to medium-sized business, you have just lost one of your key staff and you have to find a replacement.

Like everybody else, you prefer a hassle-free existence —hiring and firing people isn't your thing. You know that hiring is always a problem because if you use a recruitment service there are substantial fees to pay. But if you decide to find the person yourself there is the time-consuming process of creating the advertisements, screening all the applications, interviewing those who appear promising, making a final decision and then writing "sorry" letters to all those who missed out.

That can take weeks of your valuable time and, after it's all been done, there is no guarantee the person you choose will be suitable for the job. After a few months you might have to terminate their employment and start the whole time-consuming process all over again.

You know that firing a person is also difficult because few people are so bad that their behaviour warrants instant dismissal. Usually the performance is not quite as good as you hoped and, despite counselling and training, the feeling slowly but surely grows inside of you that this person is not suited for the job. Finally you decide they should go but your emotions get in the way (it may be their first job or they may be supporting a family) and you keep putting it off.

Eventually, after several months of internal strain, you take action or, if you are lucky, they leave and go elsewhere.

Of course, there is another way to approach the problem and it's one that many market leaders like Procter &

Gamble use. That is, to select the replacement from the ranks of your existing staff members if possible.

As the proverb says, "The devil you know is better than the devil you don't", and you could save so much valuable time if you could look around your existing staff-base to see if one of them is suitable. Naturally, you would eliminate the stirrers, the latecomers, the procrastinators, those who spend half their time playing on their phone, and those who are more interested in themselves than your business. However, amongst your own people you will usually find that rare gem who does go the extra mile, who is keen to develop their skills and who is both competent and pleasant to work with. You might not give them the job immediately, but you will offer it to them on a temporary basis to see how they handle it. Usually they do it well and then you have made two people happy—yourself and the staff member who got the promotion.

In most companies there are people leaving regularly. This happens for many reasons that may include transfer of a spouse, a decision to start a family, failure to perform, travel, ill health or a better offer elsewhere. If you do what we have taught you in this book, you will be the one in the running for the promotion when the chance inevitably comes.

Why earn more money?

It takes hard work and time to earn more money and many of you will be asking yourselves if the price is worth paying. Only you can answer that, but we urge you to give the question more than a passing thought before you give a negative answer. What do you honestly feel deep down? Do you lack the drive to do what needs to be done or are you frightened that you will do all the work and still not get the rewards? Do you doubt your own ability?

These are complex questions but a way to help find the right answer for you is to ask yourself what you would do if you won $10 million dollars today. If thoughts of a big home, exotic trips and expensive cars come to mind immediately, you do have a desire for material things. Any lack of motivation on your part is due to self-doubt or not knowing where to start. By the time you finish this book you will know where to start. Provided you make a start on your goals and your self-development program, there is no reason why you should not succeed.

Remember that earning more money will assist you to do the things you want to do and have the things you want to have. It will also help you in three important areas:

(1) You will have more money to invest, which means you will attain financial independence at an earlier age.

(2) It will provide a higher standard of living so you will have more money to spend each week.

(3) The skills you develop to earn the extra money will also assist you to reach your full potential, which we believe is your duty. Acquiring these skills will enable you to take advantage of many other valuable opportunities in the future.

The amount of money you earn is a reward for the service you give. The amount of money you have is a product of the techniques you use for retaining it and making it grow. Combine the skills of earning and investing, and financial independence is assured.

Key points:

- The amount you are paid depends on the demand for your services, how well you perform and the difficulty of replacing you.

- Markets operate on supply and demand — the more people there are seeking the same kind of work, the lower the pay is likely to be.

- When you are starting out, there is just no substitute for putting in the time, working on your skills, and making yourself a person of value to those around you.

- Make the right impression. Be the one who puts in the effort, arrives early, stays late, and offers to help out where possible.

- The amount of money you have is a product of the techniques you use for retaining it and making it grow. Combine the skills of earning and investing and financial independence is assured.

24

Go for profits not wages

*There is no security on this earth;
there is only opportunity.*
General Douglas MacArthur

If you've got this far you should be aware that we believe a happy and successful life means you are in control of it. Now we'll explain why one of the best ways to be in control is for you to have your own business.

Don't let your eyes glaze over and say, "Who, me? Own my own business!?" If you follow the principles in this book, you will be way ahead of "most people" and ultimately you will be able to achieve any realistic goals you set. Therefore, moving towards a position where you can start your own business should not be nearly as scary as it may sound.

But first, a word of warning — we promised you a happy and fulfilled life, not one that was hassle-free. If you run a business, you will still have plenty of hassles because you will be at the mercy of your customers, your staff, the bank manager, suppliers, economic cycles and every branch of government. We think it's worth it, but we do understand it's not for everybody.

Benefits of having your own business:

- You will have much more freedom
- You control your own income
- You can be flexible with your time and choose what hours you work
- You can choose when you want to have holidays
- You decide the ultimate direction of the company
- You are your own boss.

It is also one of the best ways to use the skills you have gained by personal development because you will succeed or fail on your merits.

If you are not too comfortable with the idea of succeeding or failing on your merits, you have missed the whole point of this book, so we will repeat it.

We believe that:

- All of us can choose success
- Success is predictable, and
- Success involves carrying out certain steps and it requires you to develop appropriate skills.

If that is not true, then it's all a matter of luck or being born to the right parents and, if **that's** true, we're all wasting our time trying to change what can't be changed!

Being in business means you are providing a service that people want. It may be: An accounting service to help individuals or companies with tax and bookkeeping, an online store that sells merchandise, a real estate agency to help buyers and sellers of property, a financial planner to guide people with their investments, a website development company offering solutions for small businesses, a doctor to help the sick, a builder to construct buildings or a personal trainer to assist people with their fitness and health goals.

We could fill this book with different services, but if you stop for a few minutes and do a quick internet search, you will be amazed at the huge range of businesses that are out there. It just proves that the only limits to new business ideas are the limits you place on your own imagination.

You have probably heard an expression that is used in financial planning circles, "The higher the risk, the higher the reward". It works for business, too, because going into business often involves taking risks. People in business usually work long hours and, when they are starting off, take on commitments such as big mortgages and long leases. They do this for the rewards of more income, the freedom of being their own boss and for the glorious feeling of being able to say, "This is my business and it will survive or perish because of my actions". They also face the possibility of losing everything they have if it goes bad.

The power of multiplying yourself

When you have your own business you can multiply your efforts by employing others. As you know, most business people employ staff and when they work out what to charge their customers they calculate the cost of materials, if appropriate, and also add a margin for staff wages and other overheads. This means the boss must make a profit out of the staff to cover the other costs of the business and to provide a profit. This is where the leverage comes in.

Imagine you are a top gardener and can earn $150 an hour. The most you can ever earn is the number of hours you work multiplied by $150. Even if you worked to the point of exhaustion for, say, six days a week for eight hours a day, $7,200 a week is the limit of your income.

However, imagine how much more you could earn if you had a team of people working for you and you co-ordinated them to make the best use of their skills combined with yours. Maybe you are supervising the job, paying your gardeners $100 an hour, your labourers $70 an hour, and juniors $50 an hour and yet are still charging out the whole job at $150 an hour. You could increase your income even further by selling products such as plants, fertilisers, sleepers and soil and making a profit on those as well. Now your income is limited only by the size of the operation you can manage and not by the hours of physical work you can do.

The founders of the giant Amway Corporation are Richard DeVos and Jay van Andel. They are both qualified pilots and started their business careers by giving flying lessons. Life changed for them when they worked out they could make far more money by selling flying lessons and hiring other pilots to give the lessons than to teach people to fly themselves. They had learned the power of multiplying themselves.

James says...

When multiplying yourself, it's worth taking the time to make sure you get it right. When done correctly, you'll not only magnify your own skills, you'll also build a team of comple-

mentary skillsets that can offer a better product/service to your customers.

It's a reality of the business world that most people simply don't have the same care for the business as the owners. However, by building an endearing relationship with your staff you can bridge this gap and instil that same passion in them, which then filters through to the customer experience.

Looking after your staff is one of the best investments you can make. In my experience, the best ways to do this are to:

(1) Lead by example so they can witness your values and your passion firsthand.

(2) Help them develop their skills so they're constantly engaged, challenged and committed to excellence.

(3) Be supportive of their dreams. Even if, at some stage, this conflicts with your business, they'll hopefully respect you enough to be honest and transparent.

(4) Create and maintain a channel for them to give feedback on how the business is performing and what they think could be done better. As your business matures, you'll likely be caught up more with the bigger picture, so having the eyes and ears of trusted staff members in tune with the trenches of your business is invaluable.

Using your initiative

Let us take you back several years when we lived on a four-hectare property. Our young friend Ben lived nearby and he had been mowing our lawns and helping us in the garden for quite some time. He was only seven when his father died tragically but this had not stopped his drive. He earned his first few dollars by mowing lawns and by finding and selling lost golf balls at the nearby golf course. When the land around us was cut up for development Ben noticed there were up to 60 workers on site at any one time. He started buying cases of soft drinks at wholesale prices, chilling them and selling them to the workers for a profit of 50 cents a can. He did this by pushing a huge wheelbarrow with an icebox full of drinks around the sites. As his sales increased, he expanded his range to include chocolate bars and sandwiches (which he paid his mother to make for him).

Ben is far more than just a delightful young man; he always goes the extra mile. Because we had quite a large property with a huge expanse of lawns and gardens, Ben continually found new areas that needed a mow or a clip.

Although we haven't spoken to Ben in a while, we have no doubt he will be a success at whatever he decides to do.

We suggest you establish a little business of your own as soon as possible in order to gain an idea and understanding of what it takes. The skills needed to run a business include marketing, pricing, arranging supplies, doing what you promise and putting up with the whims of customers. If you like the idea of selling, you could consider a multi-level marketing (a form of network marketing) operation where you will gain valuable experience and personal growth as well as making some useful pocket money.

If you don't find that appealing, you could try some casual work in a small business. This may be at the local store, at the bottle shop, night-fill at a large supermarket or even delivering brochures. The type of work is not important because at this stage the purpose of doing it is to give you an insight into the way a business functions.

After a few years working for somebody else, you could now think about a career and establishing your own business. You will also find many obvious fits, such as:

- A police officer can start a security business
- A carpenter can become a builder
- A personal trainer can start a business that provides online training programs and instructional videos
- A chef can open a restaurant and/or start an online cooking show.

Once you become experienced in your field, you will find that opportunities present themselves. Just make sure you stay true to yourself and focus on what you're passionate about.

James says...

It's never been easier to establish your authority. Several years ago, I started doing a fortnightly newsletter but I knew some people would never read it because they would rather listen to audio or watch a video. To address this, I decided to create a podcast essentially based off that newsletter where people could access the newsletter in whatever format they wished: written, audio (podcast) or video (YouTube). I started off with a cheap but pro-

fessional microphone, before expanding with some basic lighting, while teaching myself how to edit using free software Audacity. The videos were filmed on my iPhone, and I would get those episodes cut up into small clips that could be shared on social media.

The investment in this setup was minimal, but it's been a great way to add value to my audience and connect with new people who might be struggling with the problems I offer solutions for. The more episodes I record, the better I get, and the more listeners subscribe. Many of them become clients of mine. As my income from the show rises, I continue to invest back into the business so I can help more and more people.

We all have expertise we can share with others. We just need to be resourceful to create and make the best out of our opportunities, while harnessing the incredible advantages that technology offers. As you start to build an audience and learn more about what problems they face, the more solutions you can develop to solve those problems—and the more you'll be remunerated.

As this chapter comes to an end, think again about the words of General MacArthur that started this chapter off. There is no security, only opportunity. This century will bring the most extraordinary opportunities for those who are prepared for them. If you can run your own business effectively in this climate, the rewards will be there for the taking.

Key points:

- Owning your own business is a very challenging, yet rewarding, experience that allows you to be more in control of your life.

- Being in business means you are providing a product or service that people want.

- The only limits to new business ideas are the limits you place on your own imagination.

- When you have your own business you can multiply your efforts by employing others.

25

Investing the first money you make

Don't tell me what your priorities are.
Show me where you spend your money
and I'll tell you what they are.
James W. Frick

One of the most common questions young people have is how to invest the first $5,000 they've saved. It is not a question that can be answered in a couple of words because before you decide where to invest the money, you must decide what you are trying to achieve.

For example, if you are saving for a car or a house you should stick with the online accounts offered by the major lending organisations. There are no entry or exit fees, your money is available on demand, and you have no risk of loss if the stock market has one of its inevitable falls.

But, if you want that money to be the foundation of a long term investment portfolio and are prepared to leave it untouched for at least 10 years, you should consider shares or investment property.

There may appear to be a dazzling array of investment opportunities around but almost every investment falls into one of two categories—debt investments or growth investments.

When you make a debt investment you deposit money with an establishment such as a bank, building society or credit union which in turn lend it out to people who wish to borrow it. Your return is solely from the interest you receive.

When you make a growth investment you are investing your money in areas such as real estate or shares. It changes character and in some cases you may receive income (rent for property, dividends from shares) and also some capital gain.

Which category is right for you? That depends on what you are trying to achieve. There is no perfect investment that will be all things to all people so don't waste your time looking for it. Instead take the time to understand the good and bad points of each type of investment so you will be able to choose the ones that are best for you.

Debt investments

The most common form of debt investment is a bank account. When you put $2,000 in the bank you can be fairly certain that when you come to withdraw it the $2,000 will still be there, plus whatever interest it may have earned in the meantime. As a rule, there are no charges when you deposit or withdraw, but there may be bank fees for keeping the account.

Advantages:

- ✔ Certainty of the money being there when you need it
- ✔ The lack of costs for depositing and withdrawing, and
- ✔ The ability to withdraw all or part of it at short notice.

Disadvantages:

- ✘ You are liable to pay tax on the interest, and the rate of this tax will rise as your other income rises.
- ✘ Lack of capital growth. Money is only worth what it can buy, and each year this is reduced by inflation. If you left that $2,000 in the bank for five years you may then find that it would buy far less than it would buy now. This is called inflation. If you want to see it in practice, speak to your parents or grandparents about the price of goods and services when they were young compared to the prices today.

Growth investments

There are many growth investments but the most common are real estate and shares.

Advantages:

✔ The opportunity to receive a higher return overall than you would if you left your money in the bank (due to income and capital gain).

✔ Capital gains tax (the tax on the capital gain) may be taxed at a lower rate than income tax.

Disadvantages:

✘ Possibly fees to invest and withdraw.

✘ Your money may drop in value.

Let's imagine you had saved up $5,000 for a trip you wanted to take next year. You decided to invest it in shares because you heard there was a boom about to happen and there were bundles of money to be made.

The problem with growth investments is highlighted by the rule "Wherever there is a chance of a capital gain there is a chance of a capital loss". What if the market slumped suddenly (as happened in the 1987 crash, the 2007–2009 global financial crisis and the 2020 Covid-19 crash) and the value of your shares dropped by 40% or more? You could find that your $5,000 had dwindled to not much more than $2,000.

Real estate and share investments should be the foundation of any long-term investment portfolio and we are not highlighting their disadvantages to put you off placing money in these areas. Nevertheless, it is important you understand they should only be used in the right circumstances and that placing money in these areas is a long term project.

Most young people have the savings goals of a car, a house and travel. In many cases, the money for these is best placed in the interest bearing area. However, depending on the timeframe, a regular savings plan through a balanced unit trust might be appropriate.

A balanced unit trust is a pool of money, managed by a fund manager, that is invested in both debt and equity investments. The fund would normally have its money invested in interest bearing accounts, government bonds, local and overseas shares and real estate.

All earnings are not equal

When deciding where to invest, keep in mind that all earnings are not equal. The money you receive in your pay packet would normally come from your own efforts and this is taxed at normal personal tax rates. The rate of tax will depend on your country of residency, but as a general rule the rate of taxation will increase with your income.

You can also receive earnings by way of capital gain, as happens if you buy property and shares and they rise in value. The great thing about capital gain is that it is usually not taxed until you dispose of the asset, which may be many years away if you follow my advice of holding for the long term.

This is why it is so important to start building your portfolio at an early age. Far too many young, high income earners think earning the big money is all that matters — they confuse earning with building assets and, accordingly, get to age 30 with very little to show for 10 years of work.

Invest or buy a house?

Young people often wonder whether they should focus all their energies on saving for a house deposit with the ultimate aim of having their own home, or whether they should invest elsewhere. There is no easy answer because the best strategy depends on your own personal circumstances. For example, if you are only 18 and can't see yourself buying a house for 10 years, you are probably better to build a good share-based investment portfolio. You will receive income from the dividends and these will attract tax concessions in many countries, capital gains will be only lightly taxed and you will not be liable for that until you sell the shares to raise the deposit for your house.

The benefit of doing this is the experience you will get in watching the share market rise and fall. You'll also practise the strategy of dollar cost averaging (investing a set sum in the same investment every month) because you can buy shares in small parcels.

A further advantage is that over 10 years shares can provide much better returns than leaving your money in the bank where it will be attacked by inflation and you will be paying full tax on the interest.

Of course, the major disadvantage is that share prices can plunge (as in 1987, 2007 and 2020). A way to reduce the negative effects of this is to watch the balance closely as you get to within two or three years of buying your home. If you have had very good capital gains and you see the market fall by 15%, it may be time to consider cashing out to avoid further capital losses. This is a very rough rule of thumb and you should always take into account prevailing circumstances.

It is a different matter if you are older and intend to buy a house within two to three years. In this situation you cannot afford to lose any of your capital in entry or exit fees, and you certainly don't want to put yourself in a position where you will lose money if the market falls. You are much better off to stick with the online interest bearing accounts until you are ready to buy the house.

Key points:

- Before you decide where to invest, ask yourself what you are trying to achieve.
- There may appear to be a dazzling array of investment opportunities around but almost all are either debt investments or growth investments.
- Take the time to understand the good and bad points of each investment type so you can make the best personal choice.
- Real estate and share investments should be the foundation of any long-term portfolio.
- Savvy property buyers thoroughly research the property market in their area so they know where the trend is heading and can recognise a bargain.
- Good shares are not high risk if kept for the long term.
- People's situations never stay static.

26

Getting going

A mind stretched to a new idea
never goes back to its original dimensions.
Oliver Wendell Holmes

When Noel put down *Think and Grow Rich* he knew his life could never be the same again. It was as if a veil had been lifted from his eyes and he could suddenly see clearly for the first time. Our wish is that you will be now feeling this way too. If you can start to look at yourself and your life in a fresh way, you are well on the road to success.

Treat this book as a key that has opened the gate to a new path. For a while you will be like a foal on wobbly legs as you take those first hesitant steps along the way. You will fall over, you will face setbacks, and often things won't happen as you planned. However, you will slowly make progress as the habits of success take over your thinking. Like compound interest, that progress will gather speed as time passes.

There is no doubt the future will present extraordinary opportunities to those who are prepared. Our increasingly interconnected world now puts a premium on how companies are perceived in the public eye, affording significant opportunities to those who can amplify a brand's message far and wide and allow the company to seamlessly attract and retain customers.

Travel and its associated industries, such as hotels and restaurants, will continue to cry out for good staff who can quickly resolve complaints and enhance the experience of their guests, especially with the growing threat of services like Airbnb, and despite disruptions from challenges like Covid-19.

Demand for software engineers and other technical-savvy people continues to accelerate, as the shortage of specialist IT services' widens. Fortunately, education in these fields is becoming cheaper (free, in many cases) and more comprehensive, so there's no age or skill barrier to getting started.

Growing populations require ongoing infrastructure growth, and therefore the demand for skilled tradespeople will continue to boom. There will be strong demand for financial advisers, accountants and lawyers, as regulations and laws become more complex.

Online resources that ignore geographical barriers will continue to flourish. This means employers can easily and rapidly locate workers for tasks that need to be completed, and employees from all over the world can find quality work that they can do from the comfort of their own home.

There will continue to be breakthroughs in science and medicine, and there will be tremendous opportunities to provide health services to a rapidly growing segment known as our ageing population.

How far those individuals and companies servicing those areas will go depends on the decisions and expertise of the people running them.

Let's cast our minds back on what you have read to date. We started by saying we were concerned by the lack of confidence being felt by young people but pointed out that you face a unique set of challenges that also provide great opportunities for those who know how to handle them. The aim of this book is to release the potential you have inside you so as to enable you to handle these new challenges.

In the first three chapters we described the potential in all of us and tried to help you define what success is for you. Certainly success means different things to different people and you must find your own path.

We moved into the problem areas in the next chapter when we introduced the concept of "most people". They are the majority who go through life wishing and hoping things will change but never do anything positive about it except buy Lotto tickets. If you choose to be "most people" you will waste your life dreaming instead of achieving.

In chapter five we showed you the magic formula that can start a chain reaction. It starts with a belief, which will begin moving to reality when you write down the goal. However, a goal without a plan to carry it through is nothing more than a wish. Only by making plans and taking action can you get what you want.

In chapters six and seven we introduced you to the idea of reframing and to the notion of self-concept. Undoubtedly, how we see ourselves has a huge effect on our performance but we live in a generally negative world where our brains are bombarded from birth with negative images. The way to improve your self-concept is to slowly form the habit of achieving little successes so that each small success gives you the confidence to try the next one. Eventually you will start to think of yourself as a person who can solve your own problems, instead of being a victim in a world over which you have no control.

The law of sowing and reaping, covered in chapter eight, is such an obvious one that you would wonder why it needs to be mentioned at all. Yet "most people" spend their lives trying to reap the crop without planting the seed. Consequently, as Henry David Thoreau said, "The mass of men lead lives of quiet desperation."

In chapters nine and 10 we discussed the importance of goal setting and gave you three essential skills to speed your journey on the road to success. These are getting into the habit of going the extra mile, gaining some basic sales skills and learning to speak in public. A person who can do these three things has jumped into the top 5% of the population because so few will even attempt them.

Chapter 11 repeats the theme of the book — in order to have more, you must become more. We should think of life as a continual "do it yourself" process.

Chapter 12 contains the vital, but perhaps sad message, that we must fail in order to succeed because the only way to increase our value is to learn new skills. Every new skill takes pain and effort — hence the expression "No pain, no gain". We followed this by stressing the importance of having a positive mental attitude. It is well documented that those who think in positive terms achieve positive results, and that a positive mental attitude is an essential attribute of a winner.

We continued in this vein in chapter 14 by urging you to try as many new experiences as possible so as to speed up your personal development. Next came the universal laws (chapter 15), which may have appeared strange to you at first, as they are concerned with opposites. To receive, you first have to give, and often your best successes come out of your failures. In the following chapter we faced the reality that your life is in your hands, no one else's.

By this stage, you were two thirds through the book and the lessons turned to finance because money plays such a large part in our society. There is no doubt that nothing can take the place of money in the areas where money works.

These include giving you access to a better education, a higher standard of living and the ability to make more choices in your life.

Knowing about interest is essential because the proper use of interest will allow you to speed up your own wealth creation, while an over reliance on borrowings has put many people in bankruptcy. We let you into the secret of compound interest and showed you why it is important to manage your money so as to build a capital base. The best way to do this is to use a budget, which ensures that every dollar is put to its best use. In chapter 23 we urged you to consider steps that would lead to you having your own business as this is the best way to increase your income. The book finished by discussing the range of investments that are suitable for the person who is starting off.

As we finish, understand that your brain is like your body — it needs regular food and exercise to function effectively. If this book is to be of lasting value you will have to regard it as the starting point on your road to success and continue to learn more about the subject. Appendix 1 will help you build up an arsenal for constant growth in your journey through life, and Appendix 2 will give you some motivation and tools to hit the ground running.

Now may be an appropriate time to take a break and reflect on a little poem a friend of ours showed us as she was reading the manuscript. Unfortunately its origins are unknown.

> *There is an older person up there ahead of you, that you ought to know*
>
> *That person looks like you, talks like you, walks like you*
>
> *That person has your eyes, your nose, your chin and whether he or she hates you or loves you, respects you or despises you or is hungry or comfortable depends on you. You made that person.*
>
> *That is you: ten years, twenty years, thirty years from now.*

This is the final chapter in this book but we hope it will be the start of a new life for you. We can do no more than wish you good health and happiness on your road to wealth.

Appendix 1

Build a success library

by

Noel Whittaker

You are the same today as you will be in five years except for two things — the people you meet and the books you read.
Charles E. Jones.

Whenever I write, I think about a person I once met when I was doing a "book signing". Book signing involves sitting at a table in a busy street outside a book store autographing copies of your books for those who wish to buy them. To help attract a crowd, the store may hire a publicity person who, with the aid of a microphone and a large loud speaker, tries to entice people to stop and browse through the stacks of your books that cover the table. Occasionally a large group may gather around but more often almost everybody scurries by without giving you a second look.

The book signing I particularly remember took place at noon in Brisbane when I was signing copies of *Making Money Made Simple*. A young man walking by stopped to look at the book. He carried a pie and a can of Coke and he had a packet of cigarettes stuffed into a pocket on his sleeve. Obviously he worked on a nearby building site and there was an openness about him that appealed to me immediately.

He looked me up and down, put down the Coke, and picked up one of my books. Then he said with a smile, "Do you reckon I could read this?" "Yes, I reckon you could read it," I replied. We had a bit of a chat about earning and spending money and then he carried the book to the counter to pay for it. As he left he said, "You know, I've never read a book."

Can you imagine how I felt? Jim Rohn had taught me, "We are all affected by the books we haven't read" and I am a fervent believer in the power of books to change lives.

I thought, "What a responsibility I have. If he reads that book it may well change his life. Even if it doesn't, it might encourage him to read other books that may be of great help to him. If he finds my book boring, or heavy going, he probably won't finish it. Worse still, he may never pick up another book again."

Now you know why I write the way I do. Whenever I am reviewing what I have written I see that young man in my mind and think, "Will he understand this?"

Just as a car needs fuel, so does your mind need continual doses of motivation and knowledge. This book will show you where the road starts but it will be of little lasting benefit to you unless you keep widening your knowledge.

The power of books

You have probably had older people say to you, "I wish I was your age and knew what I know now". Well, you won't need to say that when you're their age because you have access to much of the knowledge that older people have taken a lifetime to accumulate. Through books and other material such as videos, audiobooks and podcasts you can be young and know what they know now.

You can tap into some of the greatest minds that ever lived merely by going to a library or a book store, or spending a few minutes searching for articles on the internet. At one stage Og Mandino, who is now a famous writer, had bought a $30 revolver and was about to kill himself. However something inside him made him pause and search for answers instead. He writes:

> I was just about as complete a failure as one can become. I began to spend a good deal of time in libraries looking for some answers. Where had I gone wrong? Was it too late for me? I found all the answers I needed in that golden vein of ore that every library has, that special shelf of books devoted to success, how to achieve it and how to hold on to it after one attains it. My counsellors were some of the wisest people who ever lived...people like Elbert Hubbard, Norman Vincent Peale, W. Clement Stone, Napoleon Hill, Dale Carnegie, Maxwell Maltz, Louis Binstock and Dorethea Brande. The advice from their books helped to change my life.

******

In this section I will show you how to start a success library by recommending 10 books. Countless leaders have mentioned how frequently they turned to books for inspiration when they were faced with a business or life challenge, or simply wanted to learn from some of the best teachers history has ever seen. When you develop the habit of reading (or listening to audiobooks), you will quickly discover what works for you and what doesn't.

These books are easy to read and packed with useful information. Don't buy them all at once. Find one and browse through it to make sure it excites you. Then, once you've bought and read it, start that process again with one of the other titles. When you have read all 10 books, you will hopefully have developed a love for self-growth and will be able to find other books, such as autobiographies, to assist with your journey.

Consider this list a foundation of classic books that have stood the test of time and will be just as useful for you as they were for me.

How to read

Earlier in this book we mentioned the Buddhist saying "When the pupil is ready the teacher will appear". Just reading this book has taken you to a new level of awareness and you will find if you read it again you will understand it better because a different you is the reader. This "new you" will look at life in a different light and see things you hadn't seen before. The higher awareness you have achieved will enable you to understand more of life in general. And your awareness will grow still further as you continue the learning process.

Find a book store or library in which you feel comfortable and get to know the staff there. They will be able to guide you into areas of special interest and suggest books and authors who may appeal to you. If you have trouble finding a good book store, ask the most successful person you know where they get their books from.

Understand the awareness growing process and appreciate that a book that doesn't seem right today may well contain the answers you need in the future. When you start to put together your own library you will be amazed what will happen as you progress through life. You will be able to go to your library, select a book at random and find it contains just the answer to your problem.

When you are choosing books, watch the best seller lists in the newspapers and also look inside the front cover of a book to find the number of times it has been reprinted. If a book has been selling continually for years it is obvious that people are buying it and recommending it to their friends.

The Richest Man in Babylon by George Clason.
  The classic book on money that has been on the
  best seller lists for over 80 years.

The Greatest Miracle in the World by Og
  Mandino. This book has sold over five million
  copies. When you read it, you will know why.

Making Money Made Simple by Noel
  Whittaker. This covers the principles of finance,
  tax and investment and follows naturally from
  this book.

The 7 Habits of Highly Effective People by
  Stephen Covey. This is a great work on goal
  setting on how to get ahead.

Think and Grow Rich by Napoleon Hill.
  This book has changed millions of lives.
  It may change yours too.

University of Success by Og Mandino. This book contains excerpts from many of the leading success books that have been written over time. It will help you choose which authors you would like to read next.

How to Win Friends and Influence People by Dale Carnegie. One of the greatest books on human relations ever published.

Influence: The Psychology of Persuasion by Robert Cialdini. This is the definitive book on the sales process and is a must for anybody interested in sales.

Think and Grow Rich: The Legacy by James Whittaker. This book is the modern companion to the bestselling self-help book of all time. It shows how consistent application of a proven formula turns simple thoughts into massive action, elevating ordinary people to extraordinary success.

Millennial Samurai: A Mindset for the 21st Century by George Chanos. This great book examines the opportunities and challenges of the 21st century. It offers a path forward for those who want to lead a happy, successful, and meaningful life in what promises to be the most extraordinary period in human history.

Almost certainly, the total cost of all the books listed above would be less than $250. Just think about it. If you invested only $5 a week for one year, you'd be able to buy each of these books. You would then have one of the best success libraries in the country containing information that may be worth millions of dollars to you. It is also an asset that won't wear out and one that will bring you increasing joy as the years pass.

Appendix 2

Hit the ground running

by

James Whittaker

Every morning you have two choices: continue to sleep with your dreams, or wake up and chase them.
Unknown

Do you ever get the feeling that you could be doing more with your life than you are now?

I had that feeling for as long as I can remember, but it was only in my mid 20's when something clicked. I decided that mediocrity was boring, and anything that I tried from that point on would receive 100% of my focus for the best outcome possible. This led to a lot of angst, but ultimately a much happier and more fulfilled life where I feel like I've got my hands firmly on the steering wheel.

"Most people" have it easy. They finish their job and go home to do whatever they want, without having to worry too much about the company they work for until the following day. The downside? Someone tells you when to get to work, where you're going to work, when to take lunch, when to go home, how much you're going to be paid, what you'll be doing all day, what you need to wear, and when you can take leave. If that sounds like a fair trade-off to you, that's perfectly fine, and there are many people who are happy to live that life.

If, on the other hand, you have a burning desire for something more, there are two options.

First, you can make your ambition known to the people you work with and dedicate all your efforts to climbing the ladder of an existing business; over the long term, this will lead to more responsibility, a better salary, greater security, and more flexibility. The second option is to put everything you have into starting your own business. Both of these routes require you to work tirelessly, stand out from the pack, and make tough choices.

Those who opt for the ultimate risk and start their own business find that stress can, and will, come out of left field at any moment. Their wage will almost certainly be a fraction of what it was in their previous job (generally for at least two years, and that's even if the business can survive that long); they'll be left with the full gamut of responsibilities (from managing business development to overseeing product design to scrubbing the toilets); and spare time won't seem so spare anymore. Another important consideration is that the buck stops with them, always. If you need a loan to pay wages, or your IT server overheats at 3am, or a staff member calls in sick, or a supplier cancels an order, or any one of the infinite possibilities, it's all on you.

While other people are watching TV, at the beach, or out socialising, you'll have your nose to the grindstone. People will mock you for it, friends will turn on you, relationships will break up, but you'll develop a thick skin because you know that success is forged in the flames of discipline and you'll end up attracting other people into your life who are more supportive of your dreams.

While, yes, the risks and stress of starting your own business are significant and must be considered before you determine whether the entrepreneurial life is for you, the upside is almost too good to comprehend. You just need to nurture your business like a newborn baby and make it a success, at all costs.

Mark Cuban, billionaire tech entrepreneur and owner of the Dallas Mavericks NBA team, believes that to be a success in the business world you need to, "Work like there is someone working 24 hours a day to take it all away from you." That means giving up on a lot of things you might have enjoyed previously, including socialising, sleep, money and, of course, peace of mind.

It might be timely to mention an example I have of something that came out of left field.

In November 2014, just a few months after we setup CrossFit Torian—which was still early days so we were feeling the stress of rising expenses and building our membership from 60 people—a freak storm rolled through the city, bringing with it a torrential downpour.

Within 20 minutes of the first raindrop, water had started to fill up the gym quicker than we could have ever imagined and certainly quicker than we could disassemble the equipment, especially since I had been rostered on to open and was the only person on site. The terrible weather brought traffic to a standstill, and by the time my two business partners arrived, the gym was almost knee-high in water. All we could do was wait for the flood to stop, and then start the arduous clean-up process.

We spent the next 24 hours working frantically to restore the gym to its previous condition, with the support of our awesome members. I phoned our insurance company who, of course, informed us that they would only cover a fraction of the cost; we were also left with thousands of dollars in emergency restoration expenses, not to mention the impact the water had on the equipment. It never occurred to us that a natural disaster could bankrupt us almost overnight.

We started the process of investigating the issue so we could prevent it from happening again.

Remarkably, two weeks later, an even bigger flood swept through the gym. We couldn't believe it. Not one, but two freak disasters in as many weeks!? The second kicked us while we were down and was a tremendous hit to our motivation.

Again, we were lucky that so many people rallied to help get the place back in order. Understandably, some of our members were starting to get a little annoyed that the gym they paid for was inaccessible, while us—as owners—were left at the mercy of the weather gods, at the start of a particularly ferocious storm season. Meteorology suddenly became our main topic of conversation, and every dark cloud left us very nervous.

We later found out that the drain below the premises was blocked, and a month after that the local council was able to get the issue rectified.

Fortunately, the gym bounced back exceptionally well, becoming the largest of its type in the country and one of the largest in the world. Having a business open seven days a week, with more than a dozen staff and 400 members, brought with it a whole new set of challenges. But we relished the opportunity to make the gym a better place each day and give both members and staff a wonderful experience, while working towards our mission of being the premier provider of health and fitness in the world.

In life, you can't have the possibility of victory without the very real threat of failure. Nelson Mandela once said, "Do not judge me by my successes. Judge me by how many times I fell down and got back up again." That is how I now look at life. Every error or failure, regardless of how significant, is an opportunity to improve and advance.

Stopping to feel sorry for yourself is a terrible formula for long term success. Surrounding yourself with winners and digging in every single day is the best way forward that I have found.

We are all unique, and all have different personalities, talents and dreams. Often, we don't even know who we are or what we want until crisis or opportunity arrives. You can accelerate your journey to success by turning yourself into a person who attracts opportunities. Let me clarify that. This means you don't chase opportunities; rather, you have built yourself into a person of significant value so that opportunities seek you out.

So how does that happen? By getting focused on what you really want out of life, finding out what gets you super motivated, and building your skills, knowledge and network. Put on your happy face, go the extra mile and find your passion.

Once you get an idea that something might be right for you, strap a rocket to your ambition and enjoy the ride. Don't count on support from friends and loved ones because, as the Buddha once said, "We ourselves must walk the path" and you'll find it surprisingly lonely at times. Just remember it's a marathon, not a sprint.

In 2019, I launched the *Win the Day with James Whittaker* podcast for three reasons: first, I wanted to connect with influential and impactful people more often; second, I wanted to turn that encounter into a friendship; and third, I wanted to build my own brand in the process.

The decision to start a podcast has been one of the best decisions of my entire life. Aside from amassing millions of views, and getting me in front of more individuals and businesses that need my help, it's given me friendships beyond my wildest dreams and expertise that I never would have been able to acquire in a textbook or classroom.

The podcast became a platform that I could use to attract the right people to me and ask them whatever question I wanted, in a way that simply would not have been possible otherwise. Think about it. If you were somehow able to get the founder of a billion-dollar company on the phone — an almost impossible task to begin with — how willing would they be to drop what they're doing, meet up with you, and give you an hour of their extremely valuable time? You have a zero percent chance of making that happen.

Instead, you could launch a platform (such as a podcast), interview the most influential and impactful people in your network — and there'll be at least a few people you know who can help with that — and start to ask for introductions to people you want to be connected with. The process really is that simple, but it takes persistence to follow it consistently. Like anything new, most people give up shortly after starting because they don't receive the slew of results they wanted. Yet, in podcasting, the rewards will amplify exponentially the longer you stick with it.

If I was starting my success journey from scratch, that is the exact blueprint I would follow so I could connect with the frequency of high achievers.

To help upgrade your life, health, and career more than you ever thought possible, here are some episodes from the *Win the Day with James Whittaker* podcast you might enjoy:

Episode 130: Master Your Mind with Dr. Daniel Amen
Best for health

More and more, I'm appreciating the importance of looking after both your physical health and mental health. Unfortunately, it can be very difficult to find accurate information. In this episode with 12-time New York Times bestselling author, Dr. Daniel Amen, we go through the most important health decisions you need to make — and what type of life you'll get to enjoy as a result.

Episode 134: The Champion's Path with Dr. Jeff Spencer
Best for mindset

If you're serious about winning, you need to know what it takes to win. Dr. Jeff Spencer is not only an Olympian himself, but he's also the master coach to 40+ Olympic gold medallists and world record holders, as well as some of the most successful business leaders. In this episode, Jeff laid out both his Goal Achievement Roadmap and Champion's Ladder, which will have so many applications to your life.

Episode 107: How the Metaverse Will Change the World with Kirin Sinha
Best for confidence

If you want to connect with other people and take the action required to achieve big results, you're not going to need self-confidence. In this episode, Kirin Sinha reveals her roots as a shy kid to how she became one of the most inspiring tech founders on the planet. If you struggle with confidence, this episode is a must listen.

Episode 100: Win the Day with James Whittaker (feat. Brandon T. Adams)
Best for networking and podcasting

For the 100th episode of the podcast, I wanted to share more detail about how I turned the podcast into what it is today — and how you can start to create, manage, and leverage similar relationships. We had guest host, Brandon T. Adams, for this one, and there's a lot of extremely valuable information we share about networking, podcasting, and growth.

Episode 58: How to Scale Your Business with Greg Connolly
Best for business

In this episode, Greg Connolly shares how he turned Trifecta Nutrition into the largest organic meal delivery service in the US. At time of writing, Trifecta generates USD $120M+ in annual recurring revenue, services 200,000+ customers, and has established partnerships with globally recognised organisations such as the PGA, UFC, and CrossFit Games. The best part? He reveals exactly how he did it. If you're serious about launching or running a successful business, this is the one for you.

All of these episodes can be found on Spotify, Apple Podcasts, Audible, and wherever you listen to podcasts. If you'd like the video interviews, you can find them on YouTube.

In summary, a good starting point is to gain some clarity and focus on where you are now and where you want to be in the future. After that, you need the motivation to stay hungry and get the most out of every minute of every day. Once you're ready to explode out of the gate and show the world what you've got, you need to acquire as much knowledge as you can and build as many skills as possible, while enhancing your personal brand and greatly expanding your network.

If you need some help to do this, you can enroll in the Win the Day Accelerator that I launched in 2023 with Success Magazine. It's a detailed, affordable, and effective roadmap to achieving everything you could possibly want. You can find a link for it at my website: *https://jameswhitt.com*.

Life will throw in curveballs at every turn, but look at them as an opportunity to learn and move forward. If you can do these things regularly, your success and happiness are assured. Now, get out there and hit the ground running.

Thank you for taking the time to read *The Beginner's Guide to Wealth*. Please take a moment to pass the book on to a friend or loved one who you feel could benefit from reading it, or keep it in your success library for future reference.

If you have any feedback on your experience with the book, or on the impact it may have had on your life, we'd love to hear from you.

Best regards,

Noel Whittaker

- ✉ noel@noelwhittaker.com.au
- 𝕏 @NoelWhittaker
- f fb.com/noelwhit

James Whittaker

- ✉ james@jameswhitt.com
- 𝕏 @JWhittaker01
- f fb.com/jameswhitt
- ◎ @jameswhitt
- ♪ @jpwhit

Are you ready to win?

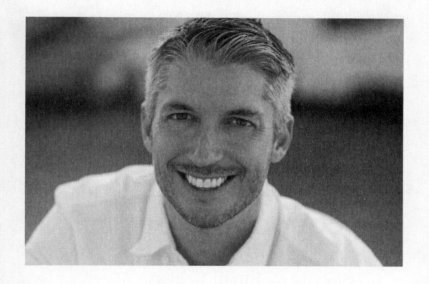

Visit James' website:
jameswhitt.com

Where you can:

- Take the Win the Day quiz
- Listen to the Win the Day podcast
- Join the Win the Day Facebook group
- Enrol in the Win the Day Accelerator, and
- Much more.

Have a large corporate order?

Email Noel at

noel@noelwhittaker.com.au

and find out about the

special offers for large orders.

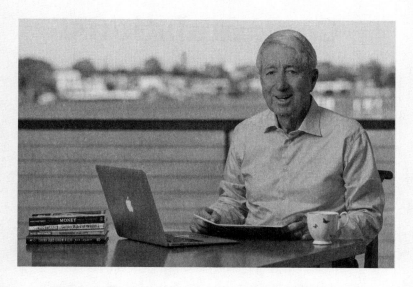

To keep up to date

with the latest financial news,
visit Noel's website at:

noelwhittaker.com.au

Where you can:

- Subscribe to Noel's regular e-newsletter
- Download his recent columns
- Buy more of Noel's products
- Ask questions relating to your financial situation, and
- Much more.

Congratulations!

If you are ready to take the next step of your financial journey, order your copy of *Making Money Made Simple*.

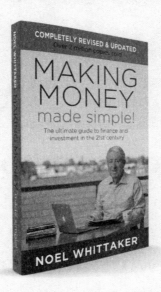

This is the most successful and influential of all Noel's books. *Making Money Made Simple* smashed sales records and sold over a million copies around the world. It stayed on the bestsellers list for a record nine years, and was voted in the Top 100 of the Most Influential Books of the 20th Century. After a complete revamp in 2020, *Making Money Made Simple* is back better than ever to teach you the essentials of money, investment, borrowing and personal finance in a way that only Noel knows how.

Index